PRESIDENTIAL PROFILES

PRESIDENTIAL PROFILES

Religion in the Life of American Presidents

by

JOHN SUTHERLAND BONNELL

THE WESTMINSTER PRESS

Philadelphia

ISBN 0–664–20897–5

Library of Congress Catalog Card No. 74–133250

PHOTO CREDITS

NATIONAL ARCHIVES
  17, 25, 31, 37, 43, 49, 67, 95, 107, 129, 135, 141, 145, 157, 165, 173, 179, 187, 193, 199, 205, 211, 217, 225, 231
  Brady Collection
  55, 73, 79, 85, 91, 101, 115, 121, 151

THE BETTMANN ARCHIVE, INC.
  61

THE WHITE HOUSE, WASHINGTON
  237

BOOK DESIGN BY DOROTHY ALDEN SMITH

Published by The Westminster Press ®
Philadelphia, Pennsylvania

PRINTED IN THE UNITED STATES OF AMERICA

PRESIDENTIAL PROFILES

CONTENTS

FOREWORD

WHEN THE AMERICAN BIBLE SOCIETY HEARD THAT JOHN Sutherland Bonnell was retiring again, this time as President of the New York Theological Seminary, it wondered whether the ebullient churchman might have time to promote the Society's Bible-reading programs. The interest of the erstwhile leader of New York City's renowned Fifth Avenue Presbyterian Church in the Bible cause was a matter of record. His tractate *How to Read the Bible* continues to be one of the most popular aids to Bible use distributed by the Society.

Indeed, Dr. Bonnell was willing. Somehow he managed to sandwich in a total of four months at the American Bible Society last year between his sacrosanct summer pilgrimage to his native Prince Edward Island with its trout streams and his insistent speaking and writing schedules. Among our several assignments which intrigued him was the one to collect and collate all the tributes paid to the Bible by famous persons of yesteryear.

This naturally led to research on a subject that Dr. Bonnell had already begun to explore, the lives of thirty-

11

six very important men, the presidents of the United States. So fascinated did Dr. Bonnell become with this segment of the study that he spent the major portion of his time those four months and almost an additional year thereafter ferreting out little-publicized and long-forgotten testimonies of how the Bible and religion helped to influence the day-to-day decisions of those who have guided the destiny of our nation these past two hundred years.

The pages following record the end result. They are a veritable compendium of heretofore scattered and lost information regarding religion's role in molding the character and guiding the statesmanship of the occupants of the White House. I can attest to the indefatigable spirit with which the researcher approached, pursued, and concluded his task. It is our hope that his studies will not only add to our storehouse of knowledge about the men we have elected to the highest office in the land, but will also put us in remembrance of how "blessed is the nation whose God is the LORD" (Ps. 33:12).

NORMAN L. TEMME
Executive Director
Education and Information Department
American Bible Society

PREFACE

AMERICANS ARE BASICALLY A RELIGIOUS PEOPLE. THEY
also expect their presidents to manifest a religious faith.
But except for a period when Roman Catholicism was
frankly regarded as an almost insuperable barrier to the
presidency, public opinion has never demanded of our
presidents any specific denominational affiliation. More-
over, when a candidate has openly avowed his intention
of running for the office, his advisers take pains to
ensure that he be photographed arriving at or leaving
a church or chapel, preferably with members of his
family.

The thirty-six men who have served this nation as
presidents have indeed been men of faith. Without a
single exception, at one time or another, they have all
publicly avowed their trust in God. This is equally true
of those who held no formal membership in any denomination. Some of the latter, such as John Adams, Abraham
Lincoln, Andrew Johnson, and Rutherford Hayes, were
profoundly religious men. President Adams, who was
renowned for his early rising, confesses in his diary
that on certain days of the week at sunrise he could be

found "studying the Scriptures." President Lincoln tells us that when the burden of his office had become too great for human strength he placed his whole reliance on God. President Andrew Johnson, Lincoln's successor, joined no church, yet was a daily reader of the Bible and used its phraseology repeatedly in his addresses. After his death this solemn declaration was found among his papers: "I have performed my duty to my God, my country, and my family. . . . Approaching death to me is the mere shadow of God's protecting wing." President Hayes made a practice of holding family worship at the breakfast table. He believed that Bible-reading had a formative influence on the character of his children.

The religious interest of these presidents, great as it may have been, was surpassed by those who had been received by baptism, confirmation, or profession of faith into church membership. It would be difficult to select thirty-six men more devout than those who are listed as our presidents from 1789 to our own time. The very nature of the presidential office with its crushing burdens, its perplexing dilemmas, its incredibly great responsibilities, brings to our chief executives an overwhelming realization that human resources and human wisdom alone are not sufficient for the task. It compels them to go for strength and guidance of that Higher Power which shapes the destinies of men and nations.

As one studies the lives of the presidents it would seem as though Providence had conspired to give them religious associations. Several of them had seriously debated entering the Christian ministry. One was actually a preacher when he was elected. Three were sons of ministers. Five had married the daughters of clergymen.

Two had served as military chaplains without ordination. One had read the Bible through three times before the age of fourteen. Half a dozen had read it at least once from cover to cover and one resolved to do this annually. One compiled a scholarly selection of the moral teachings of Jesus which was widely read at the time and is found in libraries today. Family worship had familiarized them with great passages of the Bible which remained with them through life, as President Wilson said, like the memory of a mother.

Elsewhere in this volume I have listed the books that I have found helpful in this study. It remains only for me to express my thanks to my wife, Bessie L. Bonnell, who not only read with care the entire manuscript giving me constructive suggestions but also typed 90 percent of it. To Rev. Norman L. Temme, D.D., Executive Director of the Education and Information Department of the American Bible Society, I am grateful for constant encouragement and guidance in the exacting task of research.

JOHN SUTHERLAND BONNELL

ACKNOWLEDGMENTS

ANYONE VENTURING INTO A STUDY OF THE INFLUENCE OF religion on the lives of American presidents may well be disconcerted to discover how little presidential biographers have to say on this subject; and this in spite of the fact that not a few decisions a president will have to make may well be influenced by his religious training and outlook.

Biographical material on this subject is not abundant, but if an author is willing to do a thoroughgoing job of research, he will be rewarded by instructive and sometimes exciting discoveries. The Bibliography lists the books that have proved helpful to me and I gratefully acknowledge my indebtedness to these authors and publishers for factual material.

I am grateful also for many courtesies extended me by the librarians and staff of the American Bible Society, the University Club, and the New York Public Library.

16

GEORGE WASHINGTON

GEORGE WASHINGTON

[1732–1799]

MOST BIOGRAPHERS OF WASHINGTON, WHILE REJECTING
the traditions that would make him into a "pious prod-
igy," agree that he had a firm faith in God. From a study
of his public addresses and personal correspondence one
would gather that his concept of God was not so much
a warmly personal Deity as an overruling Providence
—conceived as the Power that sustains and guides
human destiny.

Washington was born in Virginia of socially prominent parents who educated him in the Episcopal tradition. His formal school training lasted no more than
about five years. No small part of his early education
was based on Scripture and this undoubtedly contributed to the formation of his strong moral character. His
attendance was always irregular at school and he quit
in his fifteenth year. The best part of his education, however, came not from books but from his experience with
men and their outdoor occupations. Largely self-taught,
he learned surveying and rode horseback over hundreds
of miles throughout the Shenandoah Valley and beyond
it employing his skill as a surveyor. As a youth he served

in the Virginia Militia and rose rapidly in the military ranks so that at the age of forty-four he found himself commander in chief of the Continental Army.

All previous training and disciplines to which he subjected himself prepared Washington in a great hour of crisis to become the leader of the American people. That he recognized the value of the Christian faith is revealed in the fact that one of his first acts at Mount Vernon was to establish family worship. He prayed often for himself, his family, and his country. On occasions he rendered thanks to a bountiful Providence privately and publicly.

Thomas Cumming Hall, in *The Religious Background of American Culture*, says that Washington attended church without formal affiliation, that he was nominally a vestryman of the Episcopal Church. The fact has been stressed that there is no record of his taking Communion once the American Revolution had begun, but some historians have pointed out that this might have political rather than religious significance because of his earlier connection with the Church of England. Several biographical writers suggest that George Washington was profoundly influenced by the moral teachings of Jesus and that he had a firm belief in the reality and power of Providence.

The American people are inclined to be somewhat skeptical of references to God that occur in presidential proclamations, but in the case of Washington, and indeed of most all of our American presidents, there is sufficient material available in personal letters written to friends which reveal the true feelings of our presidents on the subject of their religious faith. We note with interest, therefore, the wording of a private letter written by Washington on August 20, 1778, to a Virginian friend, Thomas Nelson: "The hand of Providence has been so conspicuous in all this (the course of the war) that he must be worse than an infidel that lacks faith, and more wicked that has not gratitude to acknowledge his obligations; but it will be time enough for me to turn Preacher when my present appointment ceases."

Historians have frequently mentioned the devout manner in which Washington recited the brief oath of office during the first inauguration of a president of the United States. The ceremony was performed on Wall Street, New York, on April 30, 1789, near the place where Washington's statue now stands. Having repeated the prescribed words of his own accord, Washington added, "So help me, God," and stooping down he reverently kissed the Bible, which was held by the Secretary of the Senate.

One of the finest and most accurate estimates of the character of George Washington has come from the pen of Thomas Jefferson and reveals the impression Washington had made on Jefferson's mind during a friendship that had lasted for more than thirty years. It occurs in a letter from Monticello written to Walter Jones, who was a Virginian physician and a member of Congress. Jefferson was writing out of personal knowledge because he had served with Washington in the Virginia Legislature and again in Congress. Especially important in this connection were the four years in which Jefferson served as Secretary of State in Washington's cabinet.

He writes: "Our intercourse was daily, confidential

and cordial. . . . I think I knew General Washington intimately and thoroughly."

Here, in part, is his delineation of Washington's character: "He was incapable of fear, meeting personal dangers with the calmest unconcern. Perhaps the strongest feature in his character was prudence, never acting until every circumstance, every consideration, was maturely weighed; refraining if he saw a doubt, but, when once decided, going through with his purpose, whatever obstacles opposed. His integrity was most pure, his justice the most inflexible I have ever known, no motive of interest or consanguinity, of friendship or hatred, being able to bias his decision. He was in every sense of the words, a wise, a good, and a great man." [1]

Not only did George Washington believe that an all-wise Providence was guiding the destinies of the American people, but he firmly believed that he personally was guided and protected of God. After Monongahela, he tells of God's protective care of him as he rode through a hail of bullets, four of which tore through the coat of his uniform, and two horses were shot under him. Washington spoke of "the miraculous care of Providence that protected me beyond all human expectations." [2]

In a letter written during his presidency and quoted by an early biographer, Jared Sparks, Washington said, "There was never a people who had more reason to acknowledge a divine interposition in their affairs than

[1] Letter printed in full in Saul K. Padover (ed.), *A Jefferson Profile*, p. 227.
[2] This episode is recorded in the biography of George Washington in Bliss Isely, *Presidents: Men of Faith*.

21

those of the United States; and I should be pained to believe that they have forgotten that agency or that they failed to consider the omnipotence of that God, who is alone able to protect them." [3]

While it may well be true, as several biographers of Washington have insisted, that his relationship to organized Christianity represented by the Episcopal Church was largely nominal, nevertheless, his personal faith burned clearly and steadily. Never was this more evident than in a General Order which Washington issued from Valley Forge, May 2, 1778. It was a dark moment for the Continental Army that suffered from the disabilities of low pay, severe physical discomfort, cold and hunger, inadequate equipment, and surroundings of ice and snow. This is the General Order to his soldiers and the American people. It is a message of confident hope.

May 2, 1778

"While we are zealously performing the duties of good citizens and soldiers, we certainly ought not to be inattentive to the higher duties of religion. To the distinguished character of patriot, it should be our highest glory to laud the more distinguished character of Christian. The signal instances of Providential Goodness which we have experienced and which have now almost crowned our labors with complete success demand from us in a peculiar manner the warmest returns of Gratitude and Piety to the Supreme Author of all Good."

What further evidence could anyone demand as proof of the strong fiber of Washington's character and the courage of his soul than that he should maintain

---

[3] Quoted by Norman Cousins, *In God We Trust.*

his position at Valley Forge with an army twice beaten, ill-housed and ill-fed, and with thousands of men, as Washington himself put it, "bare-foot and otherwise naked"? As well he had to deal with a Congress that had fled into the hills of Pennsylvania and yet persisted in interfering and criticizing the efforts of Washington when it was too weak to offer him any worthwhile assistance.

As the time for his retirement drew near, Washington began to think of a farewell address. Four years earlier he had asked James Madison to draft such a message. Now that Madison was no longer in office, he turned to Alexander Hamilton. Hamilton worked on the original Madison draft and made his own changes and additions and then turned over the result to Washington for his work on a final copy. An important part of this address is given to the place of religion and morality in a democracy. This was Washington's unique contribution.

For two years after his retirement in 1797, Washington lived quietly in Mount Vernon. In December, 1799, he rode several hours on horseback through a snowstorm and returned home with a very serious cold. His physicians did little to help, for they bled him heavily four times. Also they gave him repeatedly a gargle of "molasses, vinegar and butter," and a blister of cantharides (dried beetles). His strength rapidly vanished and he faced the end in a spirit of serenity and peace. "I die hard," he said, "but I am not afraid to go. . . . Thank you for your attention, but I pray you take no more trouble about me. Let me go off quietly."

A few hours later he passed from time into eternity. The entire United States was plunged into mourning.

We in our day echo the sentiment expressed in the never-to-be-forgotten words of Henry Rea: Washington was "first in war, first in peace, and first in the hearts of his countrymen."

JOHN ADAMS

JOHN ADAMS

[1735–1826]

PRESIDENT ADAMS WAS INDISPUTABLY OF NEW ENGLAND origin, having been born in Quincy, Massachusetts, a descendant of Henry Adams. From his earliest years in public life John Adams was passionately colonial in his sympathies and in 1765 he led the protest against the Stamp Act. He was forthright, impetuous, and unflinchingly courageous, never fearing to side with unpopular as well as popular causes if he believed them to be right. These personal qualities marked him out for national leadership.

When the break with the motherland came, it was John Adams who seconded the historic resolution proposed by Richard Henry Lee: "These colonies are, and of a right ought to be, free and independent states." When the Declaration of Independence came up for adoption in the Congress, it was the inspired eloquence of Adams that ensured its adoption.

Having served the nation as minister plenipotentiary and representative of the United States Government in France, Britain, and Holland, and holding the office of vice-president under Washington, he was elected president in 1796, defeating Jefferson. He assumed the office of chief magistrate in a stormy period of increasing political intrigue. That he was competent to meet opposition and never lacked courage is revealed by an episode that occurred when he was minister to the Court of St. James, London. During an interview with the monarch, who once had been his king, George III, this ruler hinted that Adams might well feel a closer attachment to England than to France. John Adams replied, "I must avow to your Majesty that I have no attachment but to my own country." These words must have profoundly shocked the English king, coming as they did from the representative of what was still only a fledgling democracy.

John Adams, with the active encouragement of his parents, pondered seriously the question of becoming a Christian minister. His concept of God and his government of the world was much more personal than that of Washington. It was more theistic than deistic. After much heart-searching, at the age of twenty-one, he decided, somewhat reluctantly, against the Christian ministry in favor of law. But this decision would not mean a turning away from religion. In his diary, which he maintained for thirty years, he wrote: "I am resolved not to waste my time as I did last year. I am resolved to rise with the sun and to study the Scriptures on Thursday, Friday, Saturday and Sunday mornings." [1] The other mornings of the week he would devote to other studies.

His religious bent is clearly revealed in certain passages of his inaugural address: "I shall need, too, the favor of that Being in whose hands we are, who led our

---

[1] Edmund Fuller and David Green, *God in the White House*, p. 20.

fathers, as Israel of old, from their native land and planted them in a country flowing with all the necessities and comforts of life, and who has covered our infancy with this providence and our ripe years with his wisdom and power."

Adams' affinity to the Christian ministry is shown by the fact that he married Abigail Smith (1744–1818), the daughter of a Congregational minister from Massachusetts. Their eldest son became president: John Quincy Adams (1825–1829).

Abigail Adams, who was one of the most distinguished letter writers of her time, disliked the style of preaching in Congregational churches and began to attend St. Paul's Episcopal Church, New York City. Adams, too, attended Episcopal churches more frequently than those of any other denomination. The esteem in which he held Christianity in general shines forth in numerous entries in his diary, one of which reads: "The Christian religion is, above all the religions that previously existed in ancient or modern times, the religion of virtue, equity and humanity. . . . It is resignation to God, it is goodness itself to man."

After both Thomas Jefferson and John Adams had retired from public life, they reconciled their differences and began what has been described as "one of the most brilliant epistolary exchanges in history." [2] One marvels at the way in which religious themes constantly emerge in their letters and occupy a considerable percentage of the whole. One especially moving passage occurs in this correspondence in November, 1818. Thomas Jefferson learned from the newspapers that John Adams' wife, Abigail, had died, so on Novem-

---

[2] Padover (ed.), *A Jefferson Profile,* p. 183.

ber 13, 1818, he wrote him a letter of sympathy in which he told of his own bereavements. From these experiences he had learned that only time and silence would bring healing. He suggested, however, that it might be of comfort for both of them to recall that ere long they too would yield their bodies to the ground and "ascend in essence to an ecstatic meeting with the friends we have loved and lost and would never lose again."[3]

John Adams replied: "I do not know how to prove physically that we shall meet and know each other in a future state. . . . My reasons for believing it, as I do most undoubtedly, are that I cannot conceive such a being could make such a species as the human, merely to live and to die on this earth. If I did not believe in a future state, I should believe in no God. . . . And if there is a future state, why should the Almighty dissolve forever all the tender ties which unite us so delightfully in this world and forbid us to see each other in the next?"[4]

With this hope in his heart John Adams died peacefully on July 4, 1826, the most significant anniversary in all American history. On the same date and at almost the same hour his intimate and well-loved friend, Thomas Jefferson, also passed away. The absence of rapid communication at this time prevented the press from making the news of this double bereavement known for some days, but when it finally reached the public, it left the American people stunned and solemnized.

---

[3] *Ibid.,* p. 299.
[4] Quoted in Fuller and Green, *God in the White House,* p. 27.

THOMAS JEFFERSON

THOMAS JEFFERSON

[1743–1826]

FROM THE LITTLE SETTLEMENT OF SHADWELL, IN THE frontier regions of the Blue Ridge Mountains of Virginia, came one of the great liberals of modern times who was also in the front rank of the Founding Fathers. Early in life he absorbed his democratic outlook from both his frontier surroundings and the political thinking of his father, Peter Jefferson. The College of William and Mary, as well as his own personal efforts, provided him with a thorough education by the age of twenty, especially in languages ancient and modern. To this store of linguistic skill he shortly added Spanish and Italian. With these accomplishments he acquired such social graces as singing, dancing, outstanding skill with the violin and various outdoor sports. Like Washington he was a superb horseman.

In religious outlook he was closer to the ideas of Washington than to the more personal concepts of John Adams. Rarely was he willing to make any clear statement of his religious convictions. In his correspondence with a friend, Jefferson offered these pointed observations: "I have ever thought religion a concern purely between God and our consciences, for which we were accountable to Him, and not to the priests. I never told my own religion, nor scrutinized that of another. I never attempted to make a convert, nor wished to change another's creed." [1]

Nevertheless, after Jefferson had entered public life, he became the object of slanderous attacks not only in idle gossip but in the nation's newspapers. He was called atheist, spendthrift, and libertine, and accused of fraud, infidelity, and all manner of excesses. As late as 1830, the Philadelphia Public Library refused him a place on its shelves calling him an infidel. This is what was said of the president who spent his evenings for many months studying the Gospels to discover what were the basic moral teachings of Jesus. These passages he cut out of the New Testament and arranged in consecutive order. "The result," said Jefferson, "was the outlines of the most sublime system of morality which has ever fallen from the lips of man." This compilation has become known as "Jefferson's Bible."

This same Jefferson, who was accused of being a libertine and guilty of gross excesses, is the man of whom his biographer, Francis S. Philbrick, said, "He never used tobacco, never played cards, never gambled and was never party to a personal quarrel." [2]

There is no record that Thomas Jefferson ever united with any church, but he was nominally a vestryman in St. Anne's Parish, Albemarle County, Virginia. At the time that Jefferson was president, the only place for worship in the newly established city was a tobacco house that had been converted into a plain and rude

---

[1] Padover (ed.), A Jefferson Profile, p. 307.
[2] Encyclopædia Britannica, Vol. XII, p. 284.

chapel. The services were attended by half a hundred people of different denominations. During his first winter in office, Jefferson regularly attended these services. Later when preaching was permitted in the Hall of Representatives, Jefferson, during his entire Administration, was "a most regular attendant." [3]

To the end of his life Jefferson declined to identify himself with any given creed or confession. From time to time clergymen such as Rev. Thomas Whittemore, Unitarian of Massachusetts, endeavored to have Jefferson agree that his religious views coincided with those of the Unitarians, but this Jefferson resolutely refused to do. He was determined to avoid formal identification with any denomination. Nor would he do what John Adams had unhesitatingly done—give an explicit definition of what the idea of God meant to him. The nearest Thomas Jefferson ever approached to a credo was a statement he wrote in 1823: "I am a Christian in the only sense in which he (Jesus) wished anyone to be; sincerely attached to his doctrines in preference to all others; ascribing to himself every human excellence and believing that he never claimed any other."

Many Christians in our own time would find it exceedingly difficult to accept this statement as a definition of orthodox Christianity. They would specifically object to the suggestion that Jesus claimed for himself only human excellence. While Jefferson declined to accept any denominational label, he was definitely sympathetic toward Unitarianism. To Benjamin Water-

---

[3] Quoted from Margaret Bayard Smith, *The First Forty Years of Washington Society*, ed. by Gaillard Hunt.

house he wrote what may be regarded as a letter that approaches closer to religious controversy than any which came from his pen.[4] He set forth three propositions which he regarded as a summary of the doctrines of Jesus and then proceeded to contrast these with what he believed to be "the demoralizing dogmas of Calvin." Most Presbyterian apologists would insist that both of his doctrinal summaries are incorrect. Where Jefferson stands, however, is no longer left in doubt, because in the same letter he added, "I trust that there is not a young man now living in the United States who will not die a Unitarian." Jefferson's pious wish fell a long, long way short of fulfillment.

Thomas Jefferson, the greatly gifted American statesman who composed the Declaration of Independence in two days, at the age of thirty-three had placed the American people under the burden of an unpayable debt. In saying this, we think not only of the services he rendered to his country here in America but also what he accomplished in strategic capitals of Europe. Beyond this, and in another sphere of activity, we recall the enrichment he has brought to American literature by the remarkable series of letters that flowed so unceasingly from his gifted pen. How could any man write longhand eighteen thousand letters in his lifetime, not a few of them literary gems? Especially are we grateful for letters exchanged between himself and John Adams in which they opened their hearts to each other. The remaining seventeen years of Jefferson's life were spent on his estate at Monticello. "There were giants in the earth in those days," says the Bible of an

[4] Written from Monticello, June 27, 1822.

early period of human history. There were giants in America during the closing decades of the eighteenth century that witnessed the rise of the young American republic.

How extraordinary and yet entirely fitting that these two remarkable statesmen, who in their own persons typified the New America, should have said farewell to the world on the same historic day, July 4, 1826, exactly fifty years after Jefferson had written the Declaration of Independence.

When John Adams' life was slipping away, the friends at his bedside heard him whisper, "Thomas Jefferson still survives!" He did not know that a few hours earlier Jefferson had drawn his last breath when he had received an affirmative answer to his question, "Is it the fourth?"

JAMES MADISON

JAMES MADISON

[1751–1836]

ONCE AGAIN IN JAMES MADISON, VIRGINIA GAVE ANOTHER president to the United States. He was born at Port Conway, King George County, where he received his early schooling. At the age of eighteen he entered the College of New Jersey (now Princeton University) and was graduated two years later. He remained another six months studying theology and law under the direction of the college president, the celebrated educator, John Witherspoon. Madison, like John Adams, seriously thought of the Christian ministry as a vocation, and even after he became deeply involved in politics, he still continued his theological studies.

Madison has become familiarly known as "the father of the Constitution" and he fully deserves that designation. At least three notable achievements may be placed to his credit: (1) his efforts on behalf of religious freedom both in Virginia and in the country at large; (2) his contribution to the Constitutional Convention and his sponsoring of the Bill of Rights incorporated in the first ten amendments to the Constitution; (3) his service to the nation as president of the republic.

The first settlers in Virginia carried with them from England Anglican Church traditions. When settlers who gave their allegiance to other traditions began to arrive, they were met with discrimination. Baptist ministers were fined and imprisoned. Congregational ministers were forced out of Virginia. Presbyterians were religiously second-class citizens. Free-church people were taxed for the support of the state church. Madison saw at once that the very evils which the Puritans and others had crossed the ocean to escape were now beginning to flourish in the new land. Historians agree that it was chiefly the invincible logic and forceful presentations of James Madison that won the battle on behalf of Jefferson's Bill for Religious Freedom. No longer would the state be permitted to put a tax on citizens for the support of churches, or would any one denomination be able to lord it over other religious bodies. The victory won for religious freedom in Virginia would have repercussions throughout the nation and be reflected in the first amendment to the Constitution. The speeches made by James Madison on behalf of religious freedom in Virginia and throughout the nation have never been excelled and will be found profitable for reading and study in our own day and age.

Madison, like his friend and mentor, Thomas Jefferson, was reticent on the subject of his religious beliefs, especially with respect to public statements. This, he felt, was a matter between a man's own soul and God. A biographer, Bliss Isely, writes that while he attended and helped Episcopal churches financially, "he was not a communicant of any church."[1] That he had deep religious convictions cannot be seriously doubted. Like others of the Founding Fathers, he continued to give ample time to religious reading and reflection. His Christian faith was not of that otherworldly type that keeps its eyes fixed on heaven but is blind to the evils that flourish in the present world. Madison always looked hopefully toward the day when all human beings in America would be free. Sometimes he had to accept a compromise in order to make any gain at all. This contingency is seen in his authorship of the Virginia Plan, which proposed that for the purposes of taxation, slaves should be classified not as "chattels," but as "population." When it appeared that several Southern states would reject the entire proposal, Madison accepted a compromise that *five slaves be reckoned as three persons!*

Rev. Dr. John Witherspoon, the longtime friend, teacher, and counselor of James Madison, was a member of the Continental Congress and the only clergyman who signed the Declaration of Independence. His Scottish love of freedom seems also to have infected many of his students at Princeton since "nearly one-fifth of the signers of the Declaration of Independence, and an equal proportion of the convention which framed the Constitution of the United States and of the first Congress under it, were also graduates of the Princeton College."[2] Dr. Witherspoon gave tangible and public expression of his friendship and high regard

---

[1] Isely, *Presidents: Men of Faith.*
[2] William C. Rives, *Life and Times of James Madison,* Vol. I, p. 121, n. 5.

for James Madison by conferring on him the honorary degree of doctor of laws before Madison became president.

The personal correspondence which Madison conducted with friends reveals, from time to time, his profound interest in religious matters. To his friend, William Bradford, Jr. (later U.S. attorney general), he suggested that he "season his other studies with a due attention to the oracles of Divine Truth." That James Madison "practiced what he preached" is confirmed by the record of his own research. Says William C. Rives, "Among his early manuscripts which have come down to us are minute and elaborate notes made on the Gospels and the Acts of the Apostles which evince a close and discriminating study of the sacred writings as well as a wide acquaintance with the whole field of theological literature."[3]

The youthful Madison, who at the age of twenty-one wrote to his friend, William Bradford, Jr., that "my sensations for many months past have intimated to me not to expect a long or healthy life," lived to his eighty-sixth year and died peacefully in beautiful Montpelier with his beloved wife, Dolley Madison, at his bedside. We have good reason to believe that James Madison was not himself guilty of the folly against which he had warned others: that "while building ideal monuments of renown and bliss here, we neglect to have our names enrolled in the annals of Heaven."[4]

[3] *Ibid.,* p. 33.
[4] Cousins, *In God We Trust,* p. 298.

JAMES MONROE

JAMES MONROE

[1758–1831]

JAMES MONROE WAS THE FOURTH VIRGINIAN TO BECOME
president of the United States. His birthplace was located on picturesque Monroe's Creek, Westmoreland
County. At age sixteen he entered the College of William and Mary. He served in the War of Independence
as a lieutenant and took part in six battles, suffering
wounds in the battle of Trenton. After filling minor
government posts, in 1790 he became a member of
the Senate where he opposed some of President Washington's policies. After completing his stint in the Senate, he was appointed minister to France. Recalled
within two years for showing overmuch partiality to
France, he returned home. From 1799 to 1802 he was
governor of Virginia. He became governor again in
1811.

Monroe had received his legal training under Thomas
Jefferson, then governor of Virginia, and a warm friendship developed between them. Consequently, when
Jefferson became president he commissioned Monroe
in January, 1803, for several most important diplomatic

44

missions in Europe, and in April further commissioned him as the regular minister to Great Britain. These missions and responsibilities Monroe carried through with outstanding success.

With the help of the resident minister to France, Robert R. Livingston, Monroe, who had been appointed envoy extraordinary and minister plenipotentiary at Paris, succeeded in effecting what has become known as the Louisiana Purchase. Napoleon Bonaparte with the object of setting up a maritime rival to Great Britain sold the United States the vast stretch of ill-defined territory known as Louisiana. The American ministers went far beyond their instruction and settled the bargain on April 30, 1803. And bargain it was, since the new territory comprised 828,000 square miles and doubled the size of the United States. The total cost is said to have been $27,267,622, including interest charges: that is less than three cents an acre. Even the far-famed purchase of Manhattan Island from the Indians was scarcely a better bargain. No little credit for this great achievement went to James Monroe, although the burden of the negotiation fell upon the American minister, Livingston.

In 1816 Monroe was elected president of the United States by an overwhelming majority of electoral votes. In 1820 he was reelected almost by acclamation, only one electoral vote going to his opponent.

The most notable event in his career as president was the proclamation of what has become known as the Monroe Doctrine. Stated in the briefest form, it would read: "The American Continents . . . are henceforth not to be considered as subjects for future colonization by any European power."[1] This declaration in the course of the years has been given widely different interpretations and has had a profound influence on American foreign policy.

When one begins to compare James Monroe with the presidents who immediately preceded and followed him, he suffers by contrast. These presidents were towering personalities and even a man well above the average in character and ability would be dwarfed in comparison. Another handicap that Monroe suffered is in the matter of his religious practice and experience. Even a superficial reading of the biographies of the first six presidents of the United States will show that with the single exception of Monroe there is little doubt of what their religious interests and affiliations were. In the case of James Monroe neither in his public addresses nor in private correspondence does he lift the veil. Indirectly we learn that he appeared to favor the Episcopal tradition and, like several other presidents, he attended St. John's Episcopal Church in Washington. One other hint has been given us in a eulogy by John Quincy Adams. He said of James Monroe's mind that it was "sound in its judgments, and firm in its final conclusions . . . anxious and unwearied in the pursuit of Truth and right."[2] Adams was not given to distributing praise on undeserving objects. He undoubtedly saw in Monroe qualities of personality and character that are not visible to us at this so great a distance from the man in question. He was buried

---

[1] Article on James Monroe, *Chambers' Biographical Dictionary* (St. Martin's Press, 1962).
[2] Fuller and Green, *God in the White House,* p. 51.

with the rites of the Episcopal Church even as he was married by them.

The nature of James Monroe's actual relationship to his Maker—like the identity of the Unknown Warrior—is "known only to God."

JOHN QUINCY ADAMS

JOHN QUINCY ADAMS

[1767–1848]

THE ADAMS FAMILY PROVIDES THE ONE INSTANCE IN American history where a son follows his father into the presidency. Approximately a quarter of a century after John Adams relinquished his responsibilities as president of the United States his son, John Quincy Adams, assumed this same burden. His middle name, Quincy, came not from the city in Massachusetts in which he was born but from his maternal great-grandfather who also served in public life.

John Quincy Adams' training in politics began early when at the age of eleven he accompanied his father to Europe and repeated the journey two years later, studying in schools in Paris and Leyden. At this time, too, he began keeping the diary that has provided a wealth of information on his own life and the life and manners of his time. At the age of fourteen, when the average boy of today would be wrestling with his studies in high school, young Quincy Adams was journeying to Russia in 1782 as the private secretary of Francis Dana, American diplomat. Most remarkable of all, in this same year he joined his father "who was one of the American commissioners discussing the treaty of peace which concluded the War of Independence, and acted as a special secretary." In 1803 we find him in Washington serving as a United States senator.

After holding various important government posts in different countries, in 1824 John Quincy Adams was elected president of the United States. The two terms of Adams' predecessor, James Monroe, became known as the "Era of Good Feeling." The four stormy years of John Quincy Adams' presidency were quite the opposite. His term of office might well have been called the "Era of Storm," for throughout it he was under almost constant and bitter attacks from his political adversaries.

Perhaps the greatest achievement of John Quincy Adams' career came after his term as president expired. Certainly these were his happiest days. He had been elected to the House of Representatives and fought, in that body, any extension of slavery. He championed the right of slaves and others to present petitions to the House. Pro-slavery members secured the passage of a "gag rule" in 1836 to deny this right of petition. Adams fought fiercely and unceasingly to abrogate this measure and finally, in 1848, the year he died, his motion to repeal "the Twenty-first rule" was carried.

Few of the men who have occupied positions of leadership in the nation have possessed a greater measure of integrity or of personal dedication and a larger endowment of intellectual and moral capacity than John Quincy Adams.

Adams' most notable achievements both in public and private were inspired by his invigorating and infectious faith. He never lost the spiritual glow that had been kindled in his heart by the Christian home that had nurtured the formative years of his youth, the home of John and Abigail Adams. His attitude toward slavery was far more liberal than that of most of the national leaders of his day, and it was unquestionably a product of his faith in God and his divine government of the world. On one occasion Adams said that slavery was "the great and foul stain upon the North American Union."

He was a man of high standards of ethical conduct. One manifestation of this is an episode that occurred in November, 1831, while he was on his way to take his seat in Congress. While passing through Philadelphia, he called on Nicholas Biddle at the United States Bank and handed him a certificate of stock. "Sell it immediately," he said. This was not because he believed the stock was not good, for he was of the opposite opinion, but because he felt it possible that a vote might be called on some measure connected with the bank stock and therefore he ought to have no personal interest in it.[1] Adams established a pattern that might well be emulated by political leaders of our own day.

With disciplined regularity John Quincy Adams renewed his spiritual life by Bible-reading and prayer. Under the date of September 26, 1810, in his diary we read: "I have made a practice for several years to read the Bible through in the course of every year. I usually devote to this reading the first hour after I rise every morning—I have finished the perusal earlier than usual. I closed the book yesterday—I have this morning commenced it anew." Here was the fountain source of John

[1] Charles Francis Adams (ed.), *The Memoirs of John Quincy Adams,* Vol. VIII, p. 425.

Quincy Adams' inner spiritual strength and stability.

When, after his retirement, Adams was requested by the citizens of Plymouth district of Massachusetts to represent them in Congress he at once consented. Some of his friends suggested that this was a comedown for a former president. He replied: "No person could be degraded by serving the people as a representative in congress. Nor, in my opinion, would an ex-president of the United States be degraded by serving as a select-man of his town, if elected thereto by the people."

John Quincy Adams always spoke of the Independent Congregational Church as his choice of denomination, but in the absence of such a church in Washington he attended others of various denominations.

When we think of John Quincy Adams and of the inspiration and hope that he brought to the American people in the formative years of this nation's life, we gladly echo the tribute paid to the grand old man by Dr. Theodore Parker, the fiery and eloquent abolitionist of Massachusetts: "The one great man since Washington, whom America had no cause to fear."

ANDREW JACKSON

ANDREW JACKSON

[1767–1845]

ANDREW JACKSON WAS THE FIRST OF THE "LOG CABIN" presidents, having been born at the joint frontiers of North and South Carolina. Both states have claimed him, but Jackson, himself, appears to have regarded South Carolina as his native state. He was largely self-educated and had no social gifts or training. The little schooling he had was interrupted by the British invasion of the western Carolinas in 1780–1781. In the fighting during the latter year he was captured by the British. One brother was killed. The other brothers were imprisoned and contracted smallpox. One of the two died after his release.

At the time of Jackson's imprisonment an incident occurred that gave strong indication of the kind of man he was destined to become. He was commanded by a British officer to shine his shoes. Although Andrew was only thirteen at the time, he refused to obey the officer, who promptly struck him across the face with the flat of his saber. All these happenings fixed in Jackson's mind an unrelenting hatred of the British. Jackson was utterly fearless, quick to take offense as

56

his frequent duels testified, honest to the core, and always endeavoring to maintain the Christian ideals taught him by his godly, Presbyterian mother. This spare, tall, gangling, and reddish-haired youth, with a violent temper when aroused, manifested in his early teens that strong individuality and arresting personality that would both attract and repel people throughout his life. What a contrast there is between this wild, half-educated lad of the Carolinas and the fourteen-year-old John Quincy Adams attending the finest schools of Paris and Leyden and journeying to Russia as the secretary of the American minister to that country!

His training in a Salisbury, North Carolina, law office prepared him for a thriving law practice in Nashville, Tennessee. While boarding in the home of Col. John Donelson, he fell deeply in love with the colonel's daughter, Rachel. She was then at the point of securing a divorce from her husband. Believing that the divorce had been granted, they became married. Later, they learned that through a technicality the divorce had not been legally procured. Only one thing could be done: they were quietly remarried in Nashville. From that moment to the end of his life, Andrew Jackson had to defend himself and his well-loved Rachel from the ofttimes venomous insinuations of his political foes.

Jackson's interest in politics led to his election to the United States Senate in 1797. But it was, as we might well expect, in military life that Jackson's capacity for leadership really came to the fore. For ten years he had been major general of the Tennessee militia holding this post when the War of 1812 broke out and he tendered his services to the United States. Given a command in the field, he crushingly defeated the Creek

Indians and won from them twenty-three million acres of land. But his greatest achievement, and one that made him a national hero, was his amazing victory (amazing to his friends and foes alike) over a well-disciplined army of British regulars outside New Orleans on January 8, 1815, some days after the treaty of peace had been signed at Ghent, Belgium. Actually, the news of the victory reached Washington before the city heard of the Treaty of Ghent. Now Andrew Jackson—or "Old Hickory," which he was affectionately called—was an undisputed national hero.

Jackson's concept of God at this time partook of the nature of "the God of battles," a descriptive terminology he employed frequently, adding in a letter to the Secretary of War: "Heaven, to be sure, has interposed in our behalf."

When the first moves were made to push Jackson forward to the presidency, his first reaction was incredulity and opposition. Later, he changed his mind and in 1828 became president of the United States by a wide plurality. The joys of victory were sadly dimmed by the death of his beloved Rachel. His grief was overpowering. He was embittered by the realization that in some measure, at least, her illness was aggravated by the taunts and aspersions directed at her by her husband's political enemies. She shrank from the responsibility of becoming the First Lady of America, knowing that her lack of education and social training would expose her to further humiliation.

It was his love for Rachel that led Jackson into a fresh crusade—this time in defense of the daughter of dear friends, the O'Neils, who maintained a large old-fashioned tavern in Washington where Jackson and quite a few members of Congress boarded. Peg O'Neil was a "witty, pretty, saucy, and active young girl who made free with the tavern guests." Later Peg married a Major Eaton, a longtime friend of Jackson, and the president took Eaton into his Cabinet. This immediately produced a social storm. Many of the socially prominent ladies of Washington refused to meet Peg, alleging that she was little better than a strumpet. James Parton, in his three-volume *Life of Andrew Jackson*, devotes many pages to the letters, speeches, and interviews of Jackson in which he defended the daughter of his friends. All this consumed an incredible amount of the president's time and was a constant reminder of all that his Rachel had been compelled to endure.

For years Andrew Jackson regularly attended the Presbyterian Church with his wife. After her death, in fulfillment of a promise made to her, he formally joined the branch of this church which was situated back home near the Hermitage by "profession of faith." [1] This important step was not taken without preparation, because he informs us in his diary that for thirty-five years before becoming president he had customarily read three to five chapters of the Bible daily. In another entry he states that he read the Bible through at least once a year. To one of his sons-in-law he wrote, "Go read the Scriptures, the joyful promises it contains will be a balsam to all your troubles." Here, indeed, he reveals the source of that indomitable spirit with which he faced the hard realities of life.

---

[1] John Spencer Bassett, *The Life of Andrew Jackson.*

The end came for Andrew Jackson in his seventy-ninth year.[2] On Sunday, May 24, 1845, he partook of the Communion in the presence of his family. After this deeply moving ceremony, he said: "Death has no terror for me. . . . What are my sufferings compared with those of the blessed Saviour?" Later, he added: "I am in the hands of a merciful God. . . . My lamp of life is nearly out and the last glimmer has come. I am ready to depart when called."

A friend commented: "His Bible is always near him; if he is in a chair it is on a table by his side. . . . He often reads it."

He died without a struggle with his weeping friends and family around his bed. His final whispered words were: "Do not cry. Be good children and we will all meet in Heaven."

"So he passed over—and all the trumpets sounded for him on the other side." [3]

---

[2] A Mr. Wm. T. Yack, a friend of the family, kept a diary of happenings at the end. These details are found in James Parton's *Life of Andrew Jackson.*

[3] John Bunyan, *The Pilgrim's Progress.*

MARTIN VAN BUREN

MARTIN VAN BUREN

[1782–1862]

MARTIN VAN BUREN'S CHIEF TITLE TO FAME IN PRESIDEN-
tial history is the fact that he had never owed allegiance
to a British king but was born a citizen of the United
States. His father, Abraham Van Buren, was a small-
time farmer and innkeeper at Kinderhook, south of
Albany, New York. Both of young Martin's parents
were of Dutch descent. His father fought in the Revo-
lutionary War and later dabbled in local politics. Martin's education began in the little schoolhouse and later
the academy at Kinderhook. He had no college training.
Like most of our presidents he completed his legal
studies in a law office. He was admitted to the bar in
New York City in 1803 and set up a highly successful
law practice in Kinderhook.

Martin Van Buren lost no time in getting into politics.
After occupying some minor political posts, he was
elected in 1812 to the state senate. While fulfilling his
duties as state senator he had manifested unusual political skill and no little cunning. He possessed organ-
izing ability of a high order, was a leader of men, and
had many friends because of his engaging personality.

Consequently he became known as the "Little Magician."

The Abraham Van Burens, in common with their forefathers, were members of the Dutch Reformed Church. Martin's mother, so the biographers tell us, was a deeply devout woman. Martin absorbed much of her religious faith. He was esteemed a faithful churchman and was a regular attendant at religious services.

In 1821 Van Buren entered the United States Senate as a Republican and was elected governor of New York in 1828. From this time on, his rise was meteoric. He worked assiduously for the election of Jackson in 1828 and was rewarded by his appointment as secretary of state in 1829. While in this office he successfully settled disputes with Great Britain, France, and Turkey. In the latter case he secured access to the Black Sea and reciprocal commercial agreements.

In 1832 Van Buren was elected vice-president. Three years later he was Andrew Jackson's choice as a successor to the presidency and unanimously nominated at the Baltimore convention. It has been frequently suggested that this was the reward he received for his extensive and highly successful political engineering to elect "Old Hickory" to the presidency. In addition, he had stoutly defended the character of Peggy O'Neil, later Peggy Eaton, wife of Jackson's secretary of war. The self-righteous leaders of Washington's social life had united in excluding Peggy from their virtuous circle. This action placed Jackson more deeply in his debt.

Van Buren's election to the presidency in 1836 produced a majority of only 2500 votes, largely because of the assurance he had given to the electorate that he was opposed to the slightest interference with slavery even though he resisted its extension. Unfortunately for Van Buren a financial panic that became nationwide began during the first year of his presidency. It appears that during his brief diplomatic mission prior to his election as president he had purchased in London an ornate coach and had brought it back to Washington. This became a popular subject of satire by cartoonists who depicted the president as "King Van Buren" and his vehicle as the "royal coach." This was not a happy theme in a time of acute financial stringency.

There were no notable achievements in Van Buren's time in office and he gained no major distinction. The hostility and bitterness produced by the financial depression was, to a considerable degree, directed against the president himself. A parallel to this is seen in the presidency of Herbert Hoover, whose term of office coincided with the greatest depression the United States had ever known.

When Van Buren was heavily defeated in his effort for reelection for a second term he retired to his estate "Lindenwold" in Kinderhook and also traveled throughout Europe.

While living in Washington, Van Buren regularly attended St. John's Episcopal Church because there was no Dutch Reformed Church in the city. On retiring to Kinderhook, he again attended faithfully the church of his fathers.

In his inaugural address Van Buren said: "I only look to the gracious protection of the Divine Being whose strengthening support I humbly solicit and to whom I fervently pray to look down upon us all." Appealing for the blessing of Providence on "our beloved country," he concluded: "May all her ways be ways of pleasantness and all her paths be peace." (Prov. 3:17, freely translated.)

Van Buren died on July 24, 1862, at the age of seventy-nine. Bliss Isely tells us that "he always kept a Bible on the cabinet in his room for ready reference." [1]

His funeral service was one of extreme simplicity after the practice of the Dutch Reformed Church and without any of the trappings of the presidency. Only one hymn was sung and it was singularly appropriate.

> "Our God, our Help in ages past,
> Our Hope for years to come,
> Our Shelter from the stormy blast,
> And our eternal Home."

---

[1] Isely, *Presidents: Men of Faith,* chapter on Van Buren.

WILLIAM HENRY HARRISON

WILLIAM HENRY HARRISON

[1773–1841]

AFTER A PERSON HAS STUDIED THE LIVES OF THE FIRST half dozen American presidents he begins to feel like a mountain climber who has been surveying majestic peaks that tower one after another along the route of his journey. Then suddenly he finds himself in a range of foothills whose summits are dwarfed by the giant that preceded them. Because they follow so closely as they do on Washington, Jefferson, the Adamses, Madison, and other "greats" it is hard to enthuse over Harrison, Tyler, Polk, Taylor, and Fillmore. They are the foothills. Yet they too have made their contribution to American history and while it may not be as spectacular as that of their predecessors, it has helped to shape the America of today.

William Henry Harrison, born at Berkeley, Virginia, February 9, 1773, belongs to this latter class. His was the briefest presidency in our history—lasting only one month. His father, Benjamin Harrison, had occupied several important posts, including that of governor of Virginia. He was also a signer of the Declaration of Independence. William Henry had the advantage of a

68

good education and for a time was enrolled as a student of the College of Physicians and Surgeons, Philadelphia. He withdrew and entered the army as an ensign and rose rapidly to the rank of brigadier general. When the War of 1812 broke out he was given command of all the troops in the Northwest. In 1813 he was promoted to the rank of major general.

The previous year he had been proclaimed a hero after his victory over the forces of Tecumseh and his brother, the Indian "prophet," at the Tippecanoe River, November 7, 1811. After the outbreak of war with Great Britain, Harrison gained several victories, including the defeat of the British in the battle of the Thames, on October 5, 1813, in which Tecumseh, the able and courageous Shawnee chieftain, was killed in action.

Actually only a few hundred soldiers fought in these battles under the leadership of Harrison, yet they settled the destiny of vast stretches of territory and won the victorious general national prestige and paved the way for his election to the presidency.

The story of the massacre of the Americans by the Indians and the slaughter of the Indians by the Americans is told with lurid details by Freeman Cleaves.[1]

One result of William Henry Harrison's increasing fame as a hero of the Northwest is that he became increasingly important in political life and advanced rapidly through various governmental posts in Ohio until in 1825 he reached the United States Senate. By 1835 he was frequently mentioned as presidential timber. In 1836 Harrison ran against Martin Van Buren

---

[1] Freeman Cleaves, *Old Tippecanoe, William Henry Harrison and His Times.*

and was soundly thrashed. In 1840, however, the tables were turned. There was widespread discontent with Van Buren, and this time Harrison's supporters, who had also offered John Tyler as vice-president, resorted to political slogans and campaign songs. The cry "Tippecanoe and Tyler too" echoed throughout the United States. In the November election, 1840, Harrison was swept into office by an overwhelming majority. He took his oath of office on March 4, 1841, and one month later was dead of pneumonia brought on by exposure and fatigue.

We know all too little of the religious life and interest of President Harrison. He grew up within the Episcopal heritage of Virginia, and of his own family, and was doubtless baptized with Episcopal rites but apparently was not confirmed. He attended Hampden-Sydney College rather than William and Mary. About this time a Methodist revival was under way. It was not relished by William Harrison or his Episcopal-minded family.

Military records testify to the exemplary conduct of Harrison and his bravery throughout the entire period of his army service. That this was far from true of all troops and especially of the officers is evidenced by a statement made by General Harrison: "At least four-fifths of my brother officers died from the effects of intoxication." Also he had seen brother officers slain in duels and he fervently vowed never to employ such a method of settling a controversy.

While Harrison was still president-elect and en route to Washington one morning he was found at the Pittsburg House intently reading his Bible. He explained that this had been a fixed habit with him for twenty years: "First a matter of duty—it has now become a pleasure." [2]

Harrison was a regular churchgoer and always oc· cupied Pew 45 in St. John's Episcopal Church, 16th and H Street, Washington. He had announced his intention of becoming a communicant member at the approaching Easter session. In preparation for this ceremony he had purchased a new Bible and a prayer book. But death intervened. Despite all that the doctors could do, the medical skill of the day failed to arrest the progress of pneumonia.

As the end approached he asked that Psalm 103 be read to him. The message of quiet assurance breathed forth in this psalm brought peace to the heart of the dying president: "Bless the LORD, O my soul: and all that is within me, bless his holy name. . . . Who forgiveth all thine iniquities; who healeth all thy diseases; who redeemeth thy life from destruction; who crowneth thee with loving-kindness and tender mercies."

After the reading of the psalm President Harrison thanked the Lord for all his goodness and then seems to have been overpowered by emotion. A few minutes later the end came very peacefully. Old Tippecanoe had fought his last battle.[3]

When the news reached the papers the symbols of mourning everywhere appeared. Crepe hung from almost every door. People wept unashamedly. Even the Indians felt that they had lost a friend.

---

[2] Reported in the *National Intelligencer,* April 13, 1841.

[3] John Quincy Adams in his *Memoirs,* ed. by Charles Francis Adams, has given us a detailed account of the last hours of Harrison and of the funeral (Vol. X, pp. 456–459).

JOHN TYLER

JOHN TYLER

[1790–1862]

THOUGH JOHN TYLER'S ADMINISTRATION WAS FAR FROM eventful or distinctive, he established certain very important precedents. He was the first vice-president to be elevated to the presidency of the United States. While Tyler believed that his vice-presidential oath was sufficient to carry over into the presidency yet to make assurance doubly sure he took the presidential oath as well. Both of the precedents established by Tyler have been followed ever since in similar circumstances, including the latest instance: the succession of Lyndon B. Johnson to the presidency following the assassination of John F. Kennedy. Actually the Constitution is not clear in its phrasing. It states: "In the Case of the Removal of the President from Office, or of his Death, Resignation or Inability to discharge the Powers and Duties of the said Office, the same shall devolve on the Vice-President." [1]

The fact that the Constitution does not expressly declare that he shall *become* president was seized upon

---

[1] The Constitution of the United States of America, Art. II, Sec. 1, Para. 6.

by John Quincy Adams, who resolutely refused to recognize John Tyler as actually president.

In his diary, quoted in his *Memoirs*, Adams says, "I paid a visit this morning to Mr. Tyler, who styles himself President of the United States, and not vice-president acting as president which would be the correct style." [2] He regards Tyler's ascension to the presidency as a "direct violation of both the grammar and the context of the Constitution" only " 'the powers and the duties of the said office' are conferred." He has "more than a doubt whether the Vice President has the right to occupy the President's house, or to claim his salary, without an Act of Congress." John Quincy Adams' interpretation of the Constitution in the matter of rights of a vice-president has never been accepted. Ever since 1841 the action taken by John Tyler has been regarded as lawful precedent for all vice-presidents who have found themselves in similar circumstances.

Tyler was born at his ancestral home, in Greenway, Virginia, on March 29, 1790. He was brought up in the well-defined traditions of Virginia. His father, John Tyler, was a United States district judge and a governor of Virginia. Having completed his college training at William and Mary, young John entered his father's office and studied law, establishing a lucrative practice. Advancing rapidly in political life, he became congressman, governor of his native state, and United States senator.

Part of his traditional heritage was the Episcopal Church, by whose rites he was baptized, confirmed, married, and buried. His religious life, however, was

---

[2] Charles Francis Adams (ed.), *The Memoirs of John Quincy Adams,* Vol. X, pp. 463–464.

not a matter of mere outward observance. Although he has, to our knowledge, never written an explicit statement of his religious beliefs, there is ample indirect testimony to his faith in his practice of regular and devout habits of worship. His speeches and his correspondence both reveal a deep and intelligent knowledge of the Bible. A longtime friend and political co-worker, Henry A. Wise, former governor of Virginia, wrote of him: "He was by faith and heir-ship a member of the Episcopal Church, and never doubted divine revelation."

Because of religious and humanitarian scruples John Tyler was opposed to slavery, recognizing its immoralities and hoping that very gradually a form of emancipation would be achieved. However, he was determined that some constitutional means could be devised that would recognize the rights of the slaveholders.

During his time in the Senate his voting record showed great courage and he repeatedly opposed laws that he felt were an abridgment of freedom. Tyler fought the Force Bill, which authorized the president to use troops to enforce the law in South Carolina, claiming that it was a step toward "consolidated military despotism." This kind of independence and mettle showed up early in John Tyler's life. In the local school at Greenway one of the teachers who was something of a tyrant gained the hostility of his pupils. There was little opposition to his rule until young John Tyler took over the leadership of the students.

William Henry Harrison died on April 4, 1841, and one month later John Tyler succeeded to the presidency. Some of his political friends were jubilant in the belief that the project of a reestablished National Bank would now succeed despite the opposition it aroused. But to their annoyance President Tyler's firmness defeated their purpose.

Two years later, in an unusual accident, Tyler barely escaped death. While he was sailing on the Potomac aboard the warship *Princeton* the ship's largest gun exploded. Six men were killed, including the secretary of state and the secretary of war, and several others were wounded.

Two important happenings during the Tyler Administration were the annexation of Texas in 1845 and the Ashburton Treaty, which settled the boundary line between Maine and Canada.

Tyler's period in the presidency was under the shadow of impending civil war. He had taken a strong stand against Southern secession and worked hard to maintain the union, but he believed that the states had the constitutional right to secede. After he failed to gain renomination for a second term he was elected to membership in the Provisional Confederate Congress, thus becoming the only United States president ever to hold office in the Confederacy. He died before taking his seat. Like most well-to-do Virginians he had a labor force of seventy-five slaves on a 1200-acre plantation. His biographers say he was a just master but not a successful planter.

When John Tyler died in 1862 the United States Government took no notice of the event. Half a century later an official memorial was erected to the memory of this courageous, kindly, and undeniably honest man.

JAMES K. POLK

JAMES K. POLK

[1795–1849]

JAMES KNOX POLK WAS BORN IN MECKLENBURG COUNTY, North Carolina, on November 2, 1795. His middle name gives a clue to a part of his inheritance. Actually he sprang from Scotch-Irish stock and a robust, hardy, exuberant people they were. His parents were brought up in the traditions of Presbyterianism, but James K. Polk, because of a violent controversy among Presbyterians in an earlier generation, was not baptized until near the end of his life. For reasons that will later be apparent, the officiating minister at his baptism was a Methodist.

Polk's early education was delayed because of childhood illness, but at the age of twenty years he matriculated into second year at the University of North Carolina. At his graduation he stood in the front rank as a top scholar in both the classics and mathematics. From college Polk went on to the study of law in Nashville and to an acquaintance with the leading political figures of Tennessee. He was in demand as a speaker and was greatly assisted in his political career by his marriage to the socially prominent and charming Sarah Childress.

After Polk had become president, Sarah won admiration and acclaim as White House hostess. The more flamboyant members of Washington society, however, were somewhat abashed to learn that in conformity with her Presbyterian principles Sarah Polk served no liquor at her dinners and receptions, nor was any dancing permitted. The president reserved his Sunday for worship and quiet reading and declined to transact any state business on Sundays unless it was of an emergency nature. Even the French minister who had visited the White House just after the Polks had returned from church on a Sunday was received by a servant who asked the minister to please excuse the president since it was "his fixed rule to receive no company on the Sabbath."

One of Polk's few intimate friends was Andrew Jackson. It was Jackson's influence that promoted Polk to the United States House of Representatives, where he served from 1825 to 1839. During a period of four years he was speaker of the House. In 1839 he became governor of Tennessee.

Quite unexpectedly Polk was elected a compromise candidate to the presidency on November 4, 1844. The outstanding achievements of his Administration were the final annexation of Texas as a state of the Union and the Oregon boundary settlement by an agreement with Great Britain. The annexation of Texas brought on war with Mexico. In the peace settlement what are now known as California and New Mexico became, by conquest and by purchase, a part of the United States domain. The continental United States of America had now become nationally and internationally a recognized reality.

When President Polk assumed office he was under fifty years of age, up to that time, the youngest successful candidate in the history of the presidency. One biographer, George Clarence Robinson, wrote: "He entered the presidency a comparatively young man, full of vigor, and with the expressed zeal to serve his country to the best of his ability. He left the presidency four years later exhausted and enfeebled by the efforts he had made." [1] In the diary that Polk had kept throughout the four years of his presidency, recur again and again references to the crushing burden that unlimited executive patronage had imposed on him.[2]

From the standpoint of Polk's religious thinking an entry in his diary for November 2, 1845, is of unusual interest. On that Sunday the ladies had remained at home because of a day-long heavy rain. Attended by his private secretary he worshiped in the Foundry (Methodist) Church in Washington, D.C. The date was his birthday, which is registered in an old family Bible: 2 November, 1795. Under the 1845 date we read: "Mrs. Polk being a member of the Presbyterian Church I usually attend that church with her though my opinions and predelictions are in favor of the Methodist Church."

The preacher in the Foundry Church, on the Sunday Polk attended, chose as his text Acts 17:31: "Because he hath appointed a day, in the which he will judge the world in righteousness by that man whom he hath ordained." Polk adds that the sermon "awakened the reflection that I had lived fifty years and that before fifty years more would expire I would be sleeping with the generations which have gone before me. I thought of

[1] *Encyclopædia Britannica,* Vol. XVIII, p. 167.
[2] Milo Milton Quaife (ed.), *The Diary of James K. Polk.*

the vanity of the world's honors, how little they would profit me half a century hence, and that it was time for me to be putting my house in order."

On his fifty-third birthday, 1848, he wrote in his diary: "In four months I shall retire from public life forever—I will soon go the way of all earth. I pray God to prepare me to meet the great event."

The inauguration of General Zachary Taylor, President Polk's successor, took place on Monday, March 5, 1849. The day preceding this event President James K. and Sarah Polk exchanged farewells with the minister and members of the First Presbyterian Church. In his diary on the same evening Polk wrote of the affectionate farewells extended to himself and Mrs. Polk. "The scene was an interesting and gratifying one. We had attended worship regularly and with few exceptions almost every Sabbath during the term of my Presidency and the congregation to-day seemed to realize that they were about to part with us, and that in all probability we would never worship with them again." [3]

The last entry in Polk's diary was made on June 2, 1849. Less than a fortnight later he died at his home in Nashville. In the last week of his life he was baptized and received into the Methodist Church by Rev. John McFerrin, a longtime personal friend.

[3] *Ibid.*, Vol. I, p. 86.

ZACHARY TAYLOR

ZACHARY TAYLOR

[1784–1850]

GENERAL ZACHARY TAYLOR IN 1849 ADDED HIS NAME TO the long list of Virginians who had become presidents of the United States. Within a year of his birth, however, the whole family moved to Kentucky, where Zachary's father had been appointed Collector of the Port of Louisville.

Throughout the period of his youth Zachary did not lack excitement since his boyhood was spent on the edge of the wild frontier where Spaniards and Indians still hovered menacingly. His schooling was limited to lessons taught him by the New England tutor hired by his father. At the age of twenty-two he got his first taste of military service and liked it. Shortly thereafter he was given a commission by President Jefferson as a first lieutenant in the infantry. In Harrison's Indian campaigns he advanced in rank to captain and major. Finally he was ordered to Florida. For service rendered in the battle of Okeechobee during the Seminole War he was promoted to brigadier general.

When Texas was annexed in 1845, General Taylor was sent to defend the borders of this newly acquired territory. He marched his army of 3,000 men down to the mouth of the Rio Grande and established Fort Brown directly opposite Matamoras, which he proceeded to capture. These victories caused great rejoicing throughout America. It was not, however, until 1847 that General Taylor's reputation as a commander was soundly established. At the battle of Buena Vista, Taylor with 5,000 American volunteers defeated 21,000 Mexicans who suffered losses three times as great as his own. Now General Taylor was acclaimed a national hero and at once became a prime candidate for the presidency. One year after his great victory in Mexico, General Taylor was elected president of the United States. Obviously he had little understanding of what his duties and responsibilities would be since all his training and experience had been with the military.

Almost nothing is known about President Taylor's religious thinking or practice. His wife, however, was a devout Episcopalian and he regularly attended church with her. It was she and not the general who organized religious services in the various forts where they were in residence. The one testimony to Taylor's religious life that can carry any weight is that of his youngest daughter, Mrs. Elizabeth Bliss, who had assumed the duties of White House hostess. She said of her father: "He was a constant reader of the Bible and practised all its precepts, acknowledging his responsibility to God." There is no evidence, however, that he ever made any public confession of faith or united with any church.

James Polk, who had run for reelection and had been defeated by General Taylor, rode with him on the day of the latter's inauguration. He was astounded when Taylor remarked that "California and Oregon were too distant to become members of the Union, and that it would be better for them to form an independent government for themselves."[1] Polk concluded that Taylor was "uneducated, exceedingly ignorant of public affairs, and I should judge of very ordinary capacity."

Although some of his critics called General Taylor "uncouth," he usually put on a good appearance. He did not drink or smoke, which should have pleased his wife, Margaret Smith Taylor. Yet he did have a habit that many wives would find more objectionable than smoking: he chewed tobacco. Indeed, he was known as "a sure shot spitter." It is alleged that in all the months he spent in the White House he never once missed the sawdust box. One of his political opponents remarked that this was his major accomplishment while in office.

General Taylor was given little time in which to demonstrate his capacity or incapacity as president, for during the laying of the cornerstone of the Washington Monument on July 4, 1850, when he was exposed to great heat combined with worry concerning his duties as president, he contracted a form of cholera which resulted in his death five days later.[2]

Many people throughout the nation were truly grieved when they learned of the death of "Old Rough and Ready," as their hero was affectionately called. It was his indomitable courage, scrupulous honesty, common sense, and simplicity that brought Zachary Taylor through many formidable difficulties and dangers and made him for a brief period the leader of the American people.

President Taylor in his will, in addition to other be-

[1] *The Diary of James K. Polk.*
[2] Holman Hamilton, *Zachary Taylor, Soldier in the White House.*

quests, left to his immediate family 132 slaves with a cash value of $64,150 and a smaller group of more valuable slaves to his wife.

His last words were: "God knows that I have endeavored to fulfill what I conceived to be my honest duty."

MILLARD FILLMORE

MILLARD FILLMORE

[1800–1874]

A SPORADIC AND INCOMPLETE EDUCATION WAS ALL THAT
Millard Fillmore acquired. His schooling was broken
by various jobs he was able to obtain in Locke, Cayuga
County, New York, where he was born. He worked on
his father's none-too-productive farm, tried his hand as
an apprentice at the clothier's trade, and went to school
when he could. This occupied him until he was eighteen,
when he began to study law in a county judge's office.
His parents, Nathaniel and Phoebe Fillmore, continued
their struggle for a living, having moved to Buffalo.

Millard pursued his legal studies until 1823, when he
was admitted to the bar of Erie County. He had taught
school intermittently to help make ends meet. In 1830
he moved his practice to Buffalo, where he went actively
into politics. His meeting with Thurlow Weed marked
a turning point in his career and their association lasted
for twenty years.

With the help of Weed, Fillmore was elected to the
state legislature and later to the Congress. Henry Clay's
influence in 1848 secured the election of Fillmore as
vice-president on the ticket with General Zachary

Taylor. It now became the responsibility of Millard Fillmore, as vice-president, to preside over the meetings of Congress. The proslavery and antislavery members fought bitterly over every issue related in any way to slavery. Fillmore presided with "firmness, fairness and good humor," but there was no trace of genuine understanding or just compromise.

The sudden death of President Taylor, July 9, 1850, propelled Fillmore into the presidency. One of the most explosive issues with which President Fillmore had to deal was the Fugitive Slave Law. When it was passed, a veritable torrent of abuse from the proslavery congressmen descended upon Fillmore, yet he spared no effort to enforce this controversial measure.

When we seek to find some clue to President Fillmore's religious views we are baffled at every turn. We do know that for the greater part of his adult life he was a Unitarian. When Lincoln was journeying to Washington in 1861 he stopped in Buffalo and ex-president Fillmore was his host. Lincoln attended the Unitarian Church with him, but they did not see eye to eye politically. In 1864 Fillmore supported McClellan against Lincoln.

After Fillmore's retirement from the presidency he suffered a severe rejection by the American Unitarian Association of Boston. After he had been invited to take the chair at the annual meeting of this body the invitation was withdrawn. The abolitionist majority thought that Fillmore had compromised with slavery, so they wanted no part of him. Fillmore was deeply hurt by this unkindly rebuff and gradually separated himself completely from the Unitarian cause. After his second marriage, this time to Caroline C. McIntosh in 1858, he attended the Baptist church with his new wife. From time to time he was also seen in the Episcopal church. Beyond his attendance at worship there is scarcely a scrap of evidence in either his speeches or his correspondence that offers a clue to his more intimate thoughts on religion. Indeed, his speeches and letters as they have come down to us make him appear a rather negative and colorless personality. This, however, is not the verdict of his contemporaries.

Fillmore deserves credit for his willingness to suffer a certain measure of abasement when in 1855 he declined to accept an honorary doctorate from Oxford University on the grounds that he had no attainments, scholastic or otherwise, that would justify his receiving the degree. The historian Rhodes writes: Millard Fillmore "was strictly temperate, industrious, orderly and his integrity was above reproach." [1]

On his death March 8, 1874, his funeral service was conducted by three ministers: a Baptist, an Episcopalian, and a Presbyterian.

---

[1] Quoted in *Dictionary of American Biography*, Vol. VI, p. 382.

FRANKLIN PIERCE

FRANKLIN PIERCE

[1804–1869]

IT WOULD BE DIFFICULT TO CONCEIVE A GREATER CONTRAST between the circumstances of two contenders for the presidency of the United States than in the lives of Millard Fillmore and his successor Franklin Pierce. Fillmore's early life was a struggle against poverty and for even the rudiments of education. For Pierce by contrast life was a bed of roses. He was born in Hillsboro, New Hampshire, the son of Benjamin Pierce, later governor of the state. Three prominent academies prepared him for Bowdoin College. He was surrounded by military interests and provided with a flying start in law and politics. When only twenty-five years old he was elected in 1829 a member of the New Hampshire General Court and served in the legislature four years. Despite his youth he was elected speaker of the house for two successive years, 1831 and 1832. One year later he was elected to Congress and after two terms was sent to the Senate in 1837. He took this meteoric rise to power quite in stride.

Both Pierce and his wife found the last two years in the Senate disappointing. His wife, Jane, the daughter of the former president of Bowdoin College, Rev. Jesse A. Appleby, was sickly and disliked congressional life. She also noted that her husband was overmuch stimulated by the gay social life of Washington. Consequently, Pierce resigned from the Senate in 1842 and returned to his family in Concord, New Hampshire. There he established a reputation as a most successful lawyer, winning cases not only by his knowledge of law but also by his magnetic personality and oratory. He was popular with all segments of society.

During the Mexican War, Pierce enlisted as a private and was finally promoted to brigadier general of the volunteers. He was with General Scott in the advance toward Mexico City.

Returning to politics in 1850, Pierce again became the center of attention and was regarded as a promising candidate for the presidency. Since he had always been sympathetic toward the South, he began to draw support from that direction. Some three or four candidates became hopelessly deadlocked and Pierce emerged as the dark horse. He carried every state but four, yet his overall majority was only some 50,000.

While Pierce was occupied with the task of framing an inaugural address, the greatest tragedy of their married life occurred. It was on January 6, 1853, and the train that was to carry them on their journey toward Washington had traveled not more than a mile out of Andover, Massachusetts, when there was "a sudden snap and jar, then a violent shock as the car in which they were seated toppled off the embankment and rolled into the field below." [1] Mr. and Mrs. Pierce were

---

[1] Roy Franklin Nichols, *Franklin Pierce: Young Hickory of the Granite Hills*, p. 224.

only slightly injured, but their one living son, Bennie, was caught in the wreckage and killed. Ironically the president-elect's son was the only fatality of the accident. Pierce's biographer writes that Bennie's parents were stupefied with grief. They appeared only half alive. It was a terrible, unforgettable, and shattering experience to see their boy horribly mangled before their eyes.

Under this lowering cloud of bereavement the Pierces entered the White House some eight weeks later. The usual festivities attending the inauguration were abandoned and Mrs. Pierce never ceased to wear mourning during their four years in Washington. Undoubtedly this tragedy left both physical and mental wounds, which the Pierces carried to their graves. It may well be that Pierce's dependence on alcohol had its beginning in this tragic bereavement.

There was quite definitely a neurotic element in the religious thinking of Franklin and Jane Pierce. He believed that his son's death was probably a judgment of God on him for not having made a public affirmation of faith, and his wife concluded that God had taken away their son so that he would not distract his father from his important presidential responsibilities, a horrible and unchristian thought.

Even though Pierce had made no public profession of faith, he emphasized the more mechanical observances of religion. One instance of this was in his observance of the Sabbath. He would not even read his mail. More constructively Pierce read family prayers daily with all the servants assembled. Mr. and Mrs. Pierce attended public worship together in one or other of the two Presbyterian churches in Washington.

After the Pierces had left the White House in 1857,

and returned to Concord, New Hampshire, they both attended the local Congregational Church. Pierce had the unhappy lot of watching his nation slowly slipping toward the abyss of civil war, and he was as powerless to help as he had been while president of the United States. The minister of the Presbyterian Church in Concord, it appears, preached constantly on the theme of war. Wearied by this reiteration, Pierce began to absent himself from church.[2] After the death of his wife he began to attend St. Paul's Episcopal Church in Concord, where the minister, Rev. James H. Eames, shunned political themes. On Sunday, December 3, 1865, he was baptized by Dr. Eames and a few months later was confirmed by Bishop Carlton Chase.

Few men have been elected to the presidency so well educated and equipped for the responsibilities of the office as Franklin Pierce. And few have failed more dismally. He was handsome, genial, courteous, kind, an able public speaker, and generous to a fault. His brilliance, however, lacked profundity. He did not possess the strength of character so essential to true leadership. He became unpopular even in his home state and died in political and social obscurity.

He did, however, achieve a measure of inner peace. In 1868 he wrote to his friend Horatio Bridge, "I am driving out more or less daily and can report with more or less comfort 'Thou art my God. My time is in thy hand.'"

He died on October 8, 1869, just as a new day was dawning.

---

[2] *Ibid.*, p. 528.

JAMES BUCHANAN

JAMES BUCHANAN

[1791–1868]

TO CALL JAMES BUCHANAN A "LOG CABIN" PRESIDENT may be straining language somewhat, yet it is literally true, for his childhood was spent amid a cluster of log cabins at Cove Gap, Pennsylvania, where his parents owned a general store. His father, after whom his son was called, was of Scotch-Irish descent and managed to wrench a living out of the wilderness bordering on the Alleghenies. Later the entire family moved to Mercersburg. At once they became identified with a historic Presbyterian Church.

The younger James Buchanan was educated at Dickinson College, where he came under the powerful influence of the college president, Dr. John King, whom he adored. He was a brilliant student but a mischievous and rebellious one. Expelled for disorderly behavior, he was reinstated only through the influence of Dr. King. Later he chose law as a profession, enjoying a lucrative practice in Lancaster.

Early in his career he went into political life, beginning in the lower house of the state legislature. Five years later he was elected to Congress, where he became prominent as chairman of a committee dealing with the impeachment of a judge. In 1832 he was American representative at the Court of St. Petersburg, a post that he filled with distinction.

In 1834 James Buchanan was advanced to the Senate. Made secretary of state in 1845, he took a prominent part in negotiations dealing with the annexation of Texas, the Mexican War, and the Oregon Treaty.

President Pierce appointed him minister to Great Britain, where he enjoyed immense popularity. After he returned to the United States he was nominated for the presidency by the Democrats and elected by a comfortable margin. Few indeed among American presidents were better equipped for the office, but his Administration was a relative failure because he completely underestimated the strength of the abolitionist sentiment in the North. Actually he did not possess the sound judgment, the courage, and the self-reliance to face the slavery crisis. He tried until the last moment to retain the approval and backing of the South. He believed that slavery as an institution was morally wrong but held that Congress had no right to interfere with it in the states where it existed. He believed that this attitude would avoid a terrible civil war.

As the end of James Buchanan's term approached it became clear that war was inevitable. The election of Abraham Lincoln precipitated the outbreak. Buchanan turned over to his successor a nation torn with disaffection and disunity and retired in 1861 to his home at Wheatland, near Lancaster, Pennsylvania, where he remained until his death in 1868.

Buchanan's tragic inability to take a resolute stand on the slavery issue has beclouded the fact that he was a man of considerably more than average intelligence, unimpeachably honest, and that he rendered highly important services to his country.

James Buchanan's spiritual pilgrimage is of special interest for this study. He was reared in a Christian home in which both parents cherished and practiced their faith according to Presbyterian tradition. His mother had hoped that he might choose the ministry as his vocation, but his father, perhaps recalling his harum-scarum youth, was willing to settle for the law. The fact that James's brother had become a Presbyterian minister would help to heal the mother's disappointment.

James had not formally joined the Presbyterian Church, but he never treated religion lightly and maintained a degree of regularity with his Bible-reading and prayer. To his niece, whom he always treated as a daughter, though remaining himself a bachelor, he wrote: "My dear Harriet: If I believed it necessary I would advise you to be constant in your devotions to God. He is a friend who will never desert you." [1]

Buchanan was the only lifelong bachelor ever to occupy the White House. His reluctance to take marriage vows may well be due to a heartbreaking experience that happened as a result of falling in love with Ann Coleman, of Lancaster. In 1819 he became engaged to this young woman. Unfortunately she was influenced by idle gossip to suspect the genuineness of James Buchanan's love and broke off the engagement. Before

[1] Letter written November 4, 1851, George Ticknor Curtis, *The Life of James Buchanan.*

the close of the year Ann died rather suddenly of an obscure emotional illness. The gossip this time suggested suicide. It was a shattering experience that left its mark on Buchanan's life.

Religiously James Buchanan was a "seeker." He had great difficulty in gaining assurance that he was a fully committed Christian. While he was in Russia he wrote to his clergyman-brother: "I can say sincerely for myself I desire to be a Christian.—My true feeling upon many occasions is: Lord, I would believe; help thou my unbelief."

On one occasion when he was American minister to the British Government, Buchanan was discussing religion with an English lady who made a slighting and amused reference to prayer. Looking directly at her, he said, "I say my prayers every day of my life." [2]

While Buchanan was still president he requested an interview with Rev. Dr. William M. Paxton, pastor of the First Presbyterian Church of New York City. After closely questioning the clergyman on the meaning of a "Christian experience," Buchanan said: "My mind is now made up. I hope that I am a Christian. I think that I have much of the experience that you describe. As soon as I retire from my office as President I will unite with the Presbyterian Church." He feared that if he took this step while in office he would be branded "hypocrite."

James Buchanan occasionally would tell his friends how his well-loved mother had taught him how to pray and to read the Bible. He could never repeat the story without moist eyes and faltering voice. In September,

[2] In *ibid.*, Vol. II, p. 678.

1865, after he had made his public confession of faith and been received into the Presbyterian Church, he wrote happily to a friend: "I have become a communicant in the church of my fathers."

ABRAHAM LINCOLN

ABRAHAM LINCOLN

[1809–1865]

"FROM LOG CABIN TO WHITE HOUSE"—THESE WORDS HAVE
often been a favorite slogan of those who feel it necessary to stress Abraham Lincoln's rise from relative poverty to the highest post in the life of the American
people. Lincoln's former law partner, William H. Herndon, frequently used this phrase. After Lincoln's death
he had set himself up as the foremost authority of his
day on the life of the Great Emancipator. The one
supreme feature of Lincoln's life, according to Herndon,
was his rise from the lowest depths to the greatest
heights. To emphasize the point, he eagerly produced
supposed evidence of the dismal and sordid in Lincoln's
background. The best accredited historic scholarship
has largely refuted some of Herndon's claims.

Lincoln himself would never have tolerated these
ideas. Nowhere in his speeches or writing is a reference
to his humble origin used as a subtle appeal for sympathy. He would have scorned such a vulgar plea. The
"log cabin" emphasis has been overdone. To Lincoln,
what mattered most was not a man's origin, be it high

or low, but the quality of manhood that distinguished him. And there Lincoln shone like burnished gold!

Swiftly we shall recapitulate the main points of his early youth and his remarkable rise from a law office in a country town in Illinois to the presidency of the United States. The unhappiest time of his boyhood followed the sickness and death of his mother, Nancy Hanks. A thin and ragged lad of nine saw her buried in the Kentucky forest. The winter of 1818 was bleak and lonely. Fortunately within a year his father, Thomas, found a second wife who gave young Abraham the affection for which he hungered. Little is known of his opportunities for schooling except that they were limited and intermittent. Books were rare but wherever available were eagerly read by young Abe. At this time too he began to read the Bible. Its noble English prose lingered in his mind like a melody and was destined to enrich many of his greatest speeches.

When Abraham had reached the age of twenty-one the Lincoln family made the trek from Kentucky into Illinois and the six-foot-four-inch, rawboned youth was soon on his own and in search of employment. After trying his hand at sundry jobs with little success, he studied grammar and mathematics and then began to read law. Having passed the bar examinations in 1837, he moved to Springfield, the state capital, where he soon established a reputation as a successful lawyer. On November 4, 1842, he married Mary Todd.

The Lincolns attended Presbyterian services both in Springfield and in Washington, but Abraham never formally united with any church, though he reserved a pew in the New York Avenue Presbyterian Church,

Washington, D.C., and found in its pastor a congenial friend.

Abraham Lincoln's political activities began in the Illinois state legislature from 1834 to 1840. He spent a single term in the United States Congress from 1847 to 1849. After a five-year lapse from politics he was again drawn into the fray because of the sharp rise of interest in the slavery issue. On May 18, 1860, he was nominated for the presidency by the Republican Convention in Chicago and on November 6 was elected. On April 12, 1861, the Confederate states began the Civil War by bombarding Fort Sumter in Charleston harbor.

In his attitude toward slavery Lincoln, as president, was at first reluctant to adopt an abolitionist policy because he doubted the constitutionality of federal action. In addition, his election platform contained a pledge of noninterference with slavery within the states. Besides, he hoped to hold the border states within the Union. However, with the growing agony and misery of the war and rising antislavery tide in the North the president issued his final emancipation proclamation, January 1, 1863.

After President Lincoln's reelection in 1864 and the final defeat of the Confederacy he began to formulate his reconstruction policy for the South. He had barely commenced this task when he was suddenly cut down by an assassin's bullet in Ford's Theater on the evening of April 14, 1865.

Only after Lincoln's death was the true stature of this giant personality recognized. People remembered the woodsmen's proverb: "A tree is best measured when it is down." The entire nation was plunged into overwhelming grief and to the sorrow of many was added

110

a sense of devastating guilt for the scorn and contempt which they had once manifested toward the martyred president. In large part even the people of the secession states shared in the universal mourning.

The Confederate general Joseph E. Johnston was in conference with General Sherman when the latter was handed a decoded telegram telling of Lincoln's death. Sherman passed it over to Johnston, who was one of the ablest of Southern commanders, and then watched the general's face. Beads of perspiration stood on Johnston's brow. Then he said feelingly that Mr. Lincoln was the best friend they had and that the assassination was the greatest possible calamity to the South.[1]

From Buckingham Palace, London, came to Mrs. Lincoln a personal letter signed "Victoria Regina": "No one can better appreciate than I can, who am myself *utterly broken-hearted* by the loss of my own beloved husband, who was the *light* of my life, my stay, *my all*, what your suffering must be; and I earnestly pray that you may be supported by Him to whom alone the sorely stricken can look for comfort."[2]

From countries all over the world came messages of sympathy to the American people.

Now also came a belated recognition of the depth and spiritual power of addresses that President Lincoln had made during the course of the Civil War.

The *London Spectator*, commenting on Lincoln's Second Inaugural Address, said: "We cannot read it without a renewed conviction that it is the noblest political document known to history and should have for the nation and the statesmen he left behind him something

---

[1] Carl Sandburg, *Abraham Lincoln: The War Years*, p. 725.
[2] *Ibid.*, p. 733.

of a sacred and almost prophetic character—surely none was ever written under a stronger sense of the reality of God's government."

From a different perspective has come an unusually perceptive comment on Lincoln and the Bible: "No President has ever had the detailed knowledge of the Bible that Lincoln had. No president has ever woven its thoughts and its rhythms into the warp and woof of his state papers as he did." [3]

It would be a mistake, however, if we should think that Lincoln's awareness of God's presence was confined to the inclusive concept of his government of the world. We have ample evidence that Lincoln thought of God in warmly personal terms. To a delegation from the Baltimore Presbyterian Synod he said: "I have often wished that I was a more devout man than I am. Nevertheless, amid the greatest difficulties of my administration, when I could not see any other resort, I would place my whole reliance on God."

The life of this profoundly religious man was summed up in the verse of William Cullen Bryant:

THE DEATH OF LINCOLN

Oh, slow to smite and swift to spare,
　　Gentle and merciful and just!
Who, in the fear of God, didst bear
　　The sword of power, a nation's trust!

In sorrow by thy bier we stand,
　　Amid the awe that hushes all,
And speak the anguish of a land
　　That shook with horror at thy fall.

---

[3] William J. Wolf, *The Religion of Abraham Lincoln.*

Thy task is done; the bond are free:
   We bear thee to an honored grave,
Whose proudest monument shall be
   The broken fetters of the slave.

Pure was thy life; its bloody close
   Hath placed thee with the sons of light,
Among the noble hosts of those
   Who perished in the cause of Right.

"Now he belongs to the ages." [4]

---

[4] Words alleged to have been spoken by Secretary of War Stanton when Lincoln breathed his last.

ANDREW JOHNSON

ANDREW JOHNSON

[1808–1875]

IF EVER A MAN IN PUBLIC LIFE WAS COMPELLED BY CIR-
cumstance to face an almost impossible situation, that
man was Andrew Johnson, vice-president of the United
States at the time of Lincoln's assassination. So towering
was the personality of Lincoln, so marvelous his understanding of the American people, so masterful his han-
dling of men and his ability to turn enemies into friends
that there was in the nation no living man capable of
taking his place.

Certainly Andrew Johnson would not have been
selected for this role if the choice of a successor had
been made after the great chieftain had fallen. He had
too many defects of personality. He did not inspire
confidence. Even though he was a man of deep sympathy, he gave the impression of hardness and inflexi-
bility. He was often tactless in dealing with people—
too defensive and ill at ease. He failed to draw support
for his reconstruction programs. Indeed, his presidential
career partook of the nature of tragedy.

Perhaps his failure to command the loyalty and support of his political friends may have been due in some

measure to feelings of inferiority that continued to dog him. Like Lincoln himself he was born in poverty at the humblest social level. He was but three years old when his father, who was the breadwinner of the family, died. His mother remarried, but his stepfather brought no improvement in the family's lot. At the early age of ten years he was apprenticed to a tailor. In this situation he at least had some opportunities to learn to read and write. Six years later, with the apprenticeship over, he moved with his mother to Greeneville in eastern Tennessee, where he met and married Eliza McCardle, aged sixteen, a shoemaker's daughter. With commendable zeal he sought constantly to improve himself. Eliza, who had an average education, greatly helped. Before he was twenty-one, spurred by ambition, he began his political life by becoming an alderman and two years later mayor of Greeneville. Then in successive stages he became a member of the legislature, state senator, congressman, governor of Tennessee, and in 1857 a United States senator, vice-president in 1865, and a month later president of the United States. Here indeed was a speedy ascent into the ranks of political and social notables of the nation for the one-time tailor's apprentice and his wife. There were people in Washington and elsewhere who were fully aware of the humble beginnings of the Johnson family and on occasions even publicly reminded them of this fact. Now Abraham Lincoln would not have been troubled in the slightest degree about such matters, but evidently the Johnsons were vulnerable at this point.

Johnson carried the role of friend of the little man, chiefly the small farmers who were suspicious and jealous of the power exerted in Washington by slaveholding plantation owners. He had these humble folk firmly on his side. He frequently admonished with scorn this "damnable aristocracy."

When Johnson assumed the responsibilities of the presidency he sought to carry out the conciliatory policy which Lincoln had already manifested, but the president's assassination had provoked a vengeful feeling both in Congress and among the people. Soon the majority of Congress urged that the Southern states should be kept for a period under military government rather than be readmitted to the Union. Johnson vetoed the new and harsher laws proposed and Congress passed them over his veto. When the president removed Secretary of War Edwin M. Stanton from his post Johnson's enemies impeached him and he was brought to trial. He was acquitted by one vote. On March 4, 1869, he left the White House and the presidency an embittered and defeated man.

In 1875 his Tennessee constituents returned him to the Senate, where he made a powerful defense of his reconstruction policy. Again and again with great force he quoted the words he had used as president: "I am only trying to carry out the measures toward the South that Mr. Lincoln would have done had he lived."

Little has been said of the religious interests of Andrew Johnson because very little is known. His wife, Eliza, was a member of the Methodist Church, which he also attended with unfailing regularity. He stood unflinchingly for religious freedom and struck powerful blows at the Know-Nothing party, which sought to restrict the liberties of the Roman Catholics. He was thoroughly familiar with the Scriptures and frequently used its phrases in his speeches. Certainly his personal life was patterned on the precepts of the Bible, and all who knew him testified to the unquestioned integrity of his political career.

After Andrew Johnson's death an impressive statement was found among his papers. It read in part: "I have performed my duty to my God, my country and my family. I have nothing to fear. Approaching death to me is the mere shadow of God's protecting wing."

ULYSSES S. GRANT

ULYSSES S. GRANT

[1822–1885]

IN THE PERSON OF ULYSSES SIMPSON GRANT WE SEE THE American people turning once again to a soldier for their president. Up to this time all our presidents save one had been either army men or lawyers. The first and only exception was Grant's predecessor, Andrew Johnson.

Ulysses S. Grant was a man of strange contradictions. He helped to organize a lodge of the Sons of Temperance and wore the lodge regalia publicly. He said on one occasion: "I have been convinced that there is no safety from ruin by liquor except by abstaining from it altogether." Yet for the greater part of his life liquor was his major personal problem, and he was once forced to resign a captaincy because of "excessive drinking." To his credit, however, alcohol never fully mastered him.

In all personal business transactions Grant was the soul of integrity, yet his administration was riddled with scandals, bribery, and corruption. In none of them was Grant involved personally, but officials of the government, such as the secretary of war, and others close to the White House were implicated.

Grant wrote in his personal memoirs: "A military life had no charms for me, and I had not the faintest idea of staying in the army even if I should be graduated." Yet he remained a military man to the day of his death and it was the only career in which he was an undoubted success.

The boy from Point Pleasant, Ohio, spent his youth on his father's farm and doubtless there learned the rudiments of horseback riding that was destined to be his greatest accomplishment when he went to the military academy at West Point. While in training he gave no indication that one day he would be hailed as a military genius since in a class of thirty-nine he ranked only twenty-first.

An opportunity for military service came in the campaigns of General Zachary Taylor in the Mexican War and later under General Winfield Scott. Several times young Grant was honored by promotion for gallantry in the field. It would appear that he had at last found his true calling.

Grant's big chance however, did not arrive till the outbreak of the Civil War. He immediately offered his services to the war department as a colonel. His application was not rejected; it was ignored. Shortly after this his name came to the attention of President Lincoln, who appointed him a brigadier general. Assigned command at Cairo, he immediately won distinction by seizing, on his own initiative, Paducah, Kentucky. This was followed by battle after battle, most of which he won. He forced the Confederates to retreat steadily and when they took shelter in Vicksburg he besieged and captured the city and 30,000 prisoners. Lincoln immediately promoted Grant to the rank of major general in the regular army.

President Lincoln had been carefully watching Grant and came to see that here at last was a military leader able to bring the war to a successful close. The strong points in Grant's strategy were a willingness to fight, ability to make decisions, a bulldog determination, and a complete absence of fear.

Now Lincoln promoted Grant to lieutenant general, making him commander in chief of all the United States armies. General Grant, like Marshall Foch, believed in the principle: attack! attack! attack! Robert E. Lee's forces were steadily driven back until Richmond was taken and Lee finally surrendered at Appomattox Court House.

The story of Grant's meeting with Lee is deeply moving. Lee asked what the terms of surrender were. Grant replied: "All officers and men surrender to be paroled and disqualified from taking up arms again. All arms, ammunition and supplies to be delivered up as captured property." Grant also stated in the terms of surrender that "this will not embrace the side-arms of the officers, nor their private horses or baggage." Lee, with a grateful look, said to Grant, "This will have a very happy effect on my army." Lee had one final question: Might his private soldiers who owned horses take them home? Grant replied that this was not specified in the terms of surrender but since most of these men were small farmers and without their horses would not be able to get their crop in, he would give an order to his own officers that men who claimed a horse or mule could take the animal home. Again General Lee said, "This will have a happy effect." [1]

Lee then requested 2,000 rations for his hungry army. Grant said that he would give the order to his commissary.[2] The two great generals shook hands and went their separate ways.

Now "the officers of both sides came in great number and seemed to enjoy the meeting as much as though they had been friends separated for a long time." Union gunners made ready to fire a "great salute of triumph," but Grant forbade any sign of rejoicing over a broken enemy. He hoped that they would soon all be friends again.[3]

When a clamor was made in Congress to the effect that General Lee and his staff should be tried and punished, Lee immediately appealed to Grant. General Grant protested that full protection was given to Lee by the terms of the parole granted to him at Appomattox. That brought to an end any plans for trying Confederates on the charge of treason.

Julia Dent Grant, whom the General had married in 1848, was a member of the Methodist Church and attended services regularly. Grant never formally joined any church. Most serious biographers disregard the stories told of a supposed baptism and a last-minute conversion to membership in the Methodist Church. Among the notations of the old records of this church Grant is listed as a trustee but not as a member. It is

---

[1] Ulysses S. Grant, *Personal Memoirs*, pp. 483–484.
[2] Sandburg, *Abraham Lincoln: The War Years*, pp. 689 ff.
[3] *Ibid.*

believed that during the years when Grant would normally have joined a church he was repelled by the excessive emotionalism exhibited during revivals in the Point Pleasant region of Ohio. It was of the Holy Roller variety.

On one occasion when he was president, Grant was asked by the editor of the *Sunday School Times* to send a presidential message to this paper. He wrote: "Hold fast to the Bible as the sheet-anchor of your liberties; write its precepts in your hearts and practise them in your lives. To the influence of this book we are all indebted."

It was said of a character in Shakespeare's *Macbeth*: "Nothing in his life Became him like the leaving it."

These words could truly have been written of General Grant. In February, 1885, with the dark shadow of a cancerous death already hanging heavily over him, he began to write his two volumes of *Personal Memoirs*. With incredible courage and dogged determination, through depression, weariness, mental fatigue, and pain that was frequently agonizing, he continued to write. He was determined that his wife and family were not to be left penniless. The final pages were written within a few days of his death. Deservedly, the book immediately became a best seller and earned approximately half a million dollars.

With his family around him and his son bending over him to catch his last words he drifted into eternal peace.

General Grant had written a letter on July 2 to Dr. Douglas: "If it is within God's providence that I should go now, I am ready to obey his call without a murmur." [4]

After Grant's death when attendants had loosened

---

[4] Louis A. Coolridge, *Ulysses S. Grant*, p. 564.

his robe a locket fell out containing a strand of his wife Julia's hair. A note also was found that he had secretly carried around for fourteen days. This is how it read: "Look after our dear children and direct them in the paths of rectitude. It would distress me far more that one of them could depart an honorable, upright and virtuous life than it would to know that they were prostrated on a bed of sickness from which they would never rise alive. . . . I bid you a final fond farewell until we meet in another and, I trust, a better world." [5]

---

[5] Ishbel Ross. *The General's Wife*, p. 311.

RUTHERFORD B. HAYES

RUTHERFORD B. HAYES

[1822–1893]

A SURPRISING NUMBER OF PRESIDENTS OF THE UNITED States were born and brought up in comparative poverty. Generally this involved a struggle even to learn how to read and write. Rutherford Birchard Hayes fared otherwise. His father was a farmer of limited means who died before Rutherford was born, but fortunately for the orphan boy his uncle Sardis Birchard took over the responsibility of providing for his education. From the Norwalk Academy he went to a private school in Connecticut and finally to Kenyon College, Gambier, Ohio.

Rutherford Hayes began early to keep a diary. The spirit of earnestness that characterized his entire life showed itself in his youth. In his diary, when he was but eighteen years old, he wrote, "I am determined from henceforth to use what means I have to acquire a character distinguished for energy, firmness and perseverance." [1] This resolution fared better than most. Undeniably he achieved his purpose.

---

[1] Charles R. Williams (ed.), *Letters and Diary of Rutherford Birchard Hayes.*

A year and a half at Harvard Law School launched him on his career and for five prosaic years he practiced law in Lower Sandusky, his uncle's home. In 1850 he moved his office to Cincinnati and began to regret the previous five "wasted" years. He joined a literary club and heard such notables as Henry Ward Beecher, Edward Everett, and Jenny Lind perform. He became quite successful in his practice and saved enough money, with his uncle's help, to buy a new home and marry his longtime sweetheart, Lucy Webb. At every stage of his career thereafter Lucy's attractiveness, ability, and Christian character contributed notably to his success. They were admirably suited to each other, and their ideals and standards of conduct coincided. One illustration of this was their unswerving support of temperance.

One year after arriving in Cincinnati, Hayes entered the political arena. His chief contribution was a few speeches on behalf of Abraham Lincoln. He decided to enlist in the Civil War. His service was not particularly distinguished, although he suffered minor wounds and soon carried the rank of major general of volunteers.

By 1864 he was back in politics again, this time to find himself elected to the House of Representatives by a large majority. It was felt that he served his constituents well. Now another door was opening. He must run for governor of Ohio. He made seventy speeches but won only by a small margin. Hayes fared better in a campaign for reelection by securing a much larger majority. His reputation as a courageous administrator won him wide prestige. Once more he returned to his law practice until the bait of the presidency was dangled before his eyes.

In his diary under the date of April 4, 1875, he wrote: "Several suggest if elected governor now I will stand well for the presidency next year. How wild!" [2] Wild or not he began to work toward that very end. Win the governorship he did and so became a national figure. When the battle for the highest office of all was over, Rutherford Hayes squeaked through in a neck-and-neck race for the presidency. He received 185 electoral votes with his opponent Samuel J. Tilden getting 184.

No one is apt to claim for Rutherford Hayes the accolade of a notable administration. Yet it must be admitted that he advanced the interests of the nation by substantial and permanent gains. One of these was the withdrawal of federal troops from Southern states, bringing an end to much violence. This act and other constructive changes greatly speeded the progress of the South. He reformed the nation's customs houses, which went a long way toward eliminating corruption. The latter years of his term saw a revival of business prosperity.

It may be said of President Hayes as truthfully as of any other president who served up to that time that much of what he accomplished of solid benefit to America was inspired by the high moral and spiritual principles he espoused in his youth and from which he never swerved to the close of his life.

Hayes's day was methodically proportioned. He rose at seven A.M., then dressed and busied himself with writing till eight thirty A.M., when breakfast was served. At breakfast a portion of the Bible was read, each

---

[2] *Ibid.*, Vol. I, p. 303.

person reading a verse in turn. The Lord's Prayer was then recited in unison. In the course of the day the president used also to take time for a brief nap before dinner. Additional duties followed with bedtime at eleven P.M.[3]

To Rutherford Hayes must be given credit for holding the first hymn sing in the White House on Sunday evenings. Hymnbooks were distributed to the family and guests and all joined in well-loved hymns such as "Majestic Sweetness Sits Enthroned" and "Tell Me the Old, Old Story." It was always a time of joyous spiritual refreshment.

President and Mrs. Hayes with their young family regularly attended the Foundry Methodist Church, Washington. Mrs. Hayes was a member of this church, but her husband was not. He explained his feelings on the subject in his diary: "I am not a subscriber to any creed. I belong to no church. But in a sense satisfactory to myself and believed by me to be important, I try to be a Christian. Or rather I want to be a Christian and help do Christian work." [4]

On the Sunday before the fatal stroke Hayes wrote: "I am a Christian according to my conscience—I am content and have a feeling of trust and safety. . . . Let me be pure and wise and kind and true in all things."

How better can we bid farewell to Rutherford Hayes than with the closing words of Charles Dickens' will, which Hayes had a year before his death commended to his children: "I commit my soul to the mercy of God through our Lord and Saviour, Jesus Christ." [5]

---

[3] *Ibid.*
[4] Entry May 17, 1890.
[5] Entry March 13, 1892.

JAMES A. GARFIELD

JAMES A. GARFIELD

[1831–1881]

"A LOG CABIN IN THE WILDERNESS" FITLY DESCRIBES THE birthplace of James Abram Garfield. The lad who was destined to become the twentieth president of the United States was born in the frontier settlement of Orange, Cuyahoga County, Ohio, on November 19, 1831. This county was part of the vast territory over which the renowned Tecumseh, chief of the Shawnees, and his warriors had roamed. Some two decades earlier, with the defeat of Tecumseh, the power of the Indians had been broken, so the constantly growing number of settlers no longer lived in fear of the scalping knife.

When James was but two years old his father, Abram, died and the care of the four children fell upon his widow, the former Eliza Ballou. Even the youngest had to find work of one kind or another, and before the age of ten James was already adding to the family income by such labor as picking fruit, driving cattle, splitting wood. This left little or no time for schooling. Having tried his hand as bowsman, driver, and deckhand of a canal boat as well as at lumbering and farming, young James Garfield was stricken with an illness that precluded heavy labor in the future. He spent the next four years attending a high school. Those years were forever memorable to Garfield because of the unceasing battle he had to fight against poverty and his unwearying efforts to acquire an education. The greatest event in Garfield's life up to this time was his admission to Williams College and his contact with the famous educator Mark Hopkins, who had become president of the college. It was actually Garfield who, in 1871, at an alumni dinner in New York, coined the celebrated remark: "A University is a student on one end of a pine log and Mark Hopkins on the other." [1]

On graduation in 1856, Garfield became a professor at the Western Reserve Eclectic Institute at Hiram and later its principal. Soon thereafter he entered the political arena. His reputation as an antislavery speaker continued to grow, so that he was in constant demand. His progress was rapid. He taught in a school, served as a lay preacher with the Disciples of Christ, became a lawyer, and was elected to the Ohio senate in 1859. Again came an interruption. The Civil War engulfed the land, and Garfield volunteered, bringing with him a regiment of which he was the colonel. Typical of this eager, restless, ambitious man, he applied himself to a study of military manuals. He led his troops to victory in the battle of Middle Creek, January 10, 1862, in consequence of which he was made brigadier general. Later he was promoted to major general for gallantry at Chickamauga, 1863.

In the meantime while he was serving his country

[1] Fuller and Green, *God in the White House,* p. 143.

137

in the army he had been elected to Congress, as had happened also with Rutherford Hayes. From this point on he was committed to a political career. In 1880 he was elected to the Senate. It might be thought that Garfield had had little training or experience in politics, but the truth is that his opportunities for addressing crowds of people were greatly enlarged by his preaching responsibilities even though he had not been formally ordained.

In 1880 James Garfield went to Chicago as head of the Ohio delegation to the Republican Convention. A deadlock developed, and after a faltering beginning of the voting, Garfield got the nomination with a large majority. Then he proceeded to win the presidency. President Garfield with his customary forthrightness and integrity began an investigation and reform of both the postal and customs departments, which were filled with corruption. Tragically, however, on July 2, 1881, after only four months in office he was shot. The assassination occurred in the Washington railway station. The crime was committed by an apparently demented man, Charles J. Guiteau, a lawyer who felt it was his duty to clear the way for vice-president Chester Arthur to take the office. He was also a frustrated office seeker. When the news appeared in the press a shudder of horror passed through the nation.

President Garfield lingered on in weakness and extreme pain. His spine had been shattered, but the spinal cord was not severed. It was, however, a slowly spreading infection that ultimately brought his death. When it was learned that Garfield's wife and five children would be left in financial straits a fund was established. Garfield learned of this, and his eyes filled with tears as he exclaimed: "How kind and thoughtful. What a generous people!" [2]

On Thursday, September 8, Garfield was aroused by the ringing of church bells. "Are they praying for me?" he asked. "Yes, the people of the entire country are praying for you to-day," said Dr. Edson, who was standing by his bedside. "God bless them," replied Garfield fervently and, turning his head on the pillow, was silent a long time.[3] He lingered eleven days, dying peacefully after little more than six months in office.

When word reached his aged mother that the president had died she said thoughtfully, "He was the best son a mother ever had." [4]

---

[2] Theodore Clarke Smith, *The Life and Letters of James Abram Garfield.*
[3] *Ibid.*, p. 1199.
[4] *Ibid.*, p. 1201.

CHESTER A. ARTHUR

CHESTER A. ARTHUR

[1830–1886]

VICE-PRESIDENT CHESTER ALAN ARTHUR STEPPED INTO THE
presidency made suddenly vacant by the death of James
Garfield. Born in Fairfield, Vermont, and educated in
Union College, Schenectady, he was by no means a
stranger to New York. Arthur's reputation as a lawyer
in New York began with the famous Lemmon Slave
Case. He won a decision from the highest state courts
that slaves brought into New York in transit between
slave states were *ipso facto* free. He also won for New
York Negroes the same rights of accommodation on
the street railways as enjoyed by whites.

On the other hand, an unfavorable impression was
created respecting Arthur when he was removed from
the post of collector of customs for the port of New
York to which he had been appointed by President
Ulysses S. Grant. He was swept out of the post in the
reforms instituted by President Rutherford B. Hayes.
When James A. Garfield was elected president, as a
gesture of conciliation to the opponents of reform,
Chester Arthur was made vice-president. His nomina-

tion and election aroused little enthusiasm and some hostility.

Even in the short period that Garfield served as president he found himself in frequent conflict with Vice-President Arthur on the subject of political patronage. It should be borne in mind that no actual wrongdoing had ever been imputed to Chester Arthur, even though he had made no attempt to reform the customs service.

When the news reached Arthur that President Garfield had died he wept inconsolably. The public in general were dismayed at the prospect of living under a president who had fully approved the patronage system. This uneasiness was clearly expressed in the nation's press, which deeply hurt Chester Arthur.

Reasons for hope, however, soon became apparent. Arthur took the presidential oath twice: the first administered as soon as news of the president's death reached him and the second when the chief justice of the United States Supreme Court presided. On the latter occasion President Arthur opened the Bible at the Thirty-first Psalm and reverently kissed the page. He chose that psalm because the opening verses reminded him of the Te Deum, which his wife, who had died before he became vice-president, frequently sang in the Episcopal choir. The first verse reads: "In thee, O LORD, do I put my trust; let me never be ashamed: deliver me in thy righteousness."

Although President Arthur was the son of a Baptist minister he regularly attended the Episcopal Church but never formally united with it. In memory of his beloved wife he placed a beautiful memorial window in St. John's Episcopal Church, Washington, D.C.

President Arthur's inaugural address encouraged people to believe that despite widespread anxieties on the subject he would yet make a good president. His remarks were explicit and reassuring in that he promised an administration free of animosity and factionalism, and he lived up to the promise. The only people who were grievously disappointed were those who sought a continuation and increase of the spoils system. To one eager suppliant for patronage he said, "Since I came here I have learned that Chester A. Arthur is one man and the President of the United States is another." So does high responsibility sober and mature a man!

President Arthur heartily promoted the Pendleton law, which helped to clean up pockets of corruption in various segments of the civil service, and in so doing carried forward the reforms begun by Presidents Hayes and Garfield.

One of Arthur's most publicized acts was his dedication of the Washington Monument, in the nation's capital, which was brought to completion during his Administration.

He died on November 18, 1886, in New York City.

GROVER CLEVELAND

GROVER CLEVELAND

[1837–1908]

GROVER CLEVELAND WAS THE FIFTH IN A FAMILY OF NINE children. His father was a country minister of the Presbyterian Church. He was the second clergyman's son to become president of the United States. His father's salary never exceeded one thousand dollars a year. It is surely a tribute to the home life of the Clevelands that, despite the constant battle with deprivation, Grover's older brother, William, followed his father's footsteps into the ministry.

Robert McElroy paints a graphic picture of the preparation for the Sabbath that was unfailingly made in the Cleveland household: the tub of steaming water in the kitchen for the Saturday night bath, the preparation of a peck of potatoes and other vegetables, the readying of a roast or stew and the well-spiced pot of rice pudding. All had to be got ready the night before Sunday. When the youngsters were tucked into bed the older children went to the church to practice the hymns for the morrow's services. In such an atmosphere was young Grover Cleveland brought up. Mc-

Elroy adds, "It inevitably tended to produce a keen sense of personal responsibility, to make trust-worthy character. . . . It taught that there is a right which is eternally right, and a wrong which must remain forever wrong." [1] Grover Cleveland never ceased to be grateful for his upbringing in a minister's family. In a personal letter he wrote, "I have always felt that my training as a minister's son has been more valuable to me as a strengthening influence than any other incident in my life." [2]

In 1853 Grover's father died suddenly and the son at the age of sixteen had to forgo his plans for an education at Hamilton College, from which his brother William had just graduated, and to bear his share of the burden of providing for the orphaned family. Several unimportant jobs helped somewhat but contributed little to his own personal advancement.

During his youthful days he heard a sermon by the famous Henry Ward Beecher in the Plymouth Church, Brooklyn. Cleveland says that the inspiration of that sermon stayed with him throughout his entire life.

Then dramatically the picture changed. Grover joined the family of his mother's uncle, Lewis Allen, a cattle breeder. His home was at Black Rock in the suburbs of Buffalo. This influential relative placed him in a law office. He applied himself with such diligence that the partners and clerks on one occasion locked up the office for lunch forgetting that he was in the law library. His only comment on their return was: "Some

---

[1] Robert McElroy, *Grover Cleveland, The Man and the Statesman,* Vol. I, p. 7.
[2] Allan Nevins, *Grover Cleveland, A Study in Courage,* pp. 50–51.

147

day I will be better remembered."[3] These words were truly prophetic.

His reputation as a lawyer grew and his income increased. The fact that he had become the chief support of his widowed mother kept him out of the army when the Civil War broke upon the country. However, two of his brothers represented the family in the Northern army. While sheriff of Erie County he was of necessity involved in the execution of two murderers. These two events—military exemption and his office of executioner—were used against him in later political life. So also was the fact that he was at times overly boisterous in his recreations.

In 1881 he was elected mayor of Buffalo and the following year governor of New York. He vigorously attacked corruption in Buffalo when mayor and even more decisively did battle with crooked politicians and their supporters in New York City. Daringly he challenged the political supremacy of Tammany Hall. This manifestation of uprightness and integrity was later to stand him in good stead when he was nominated for the presidency. "We love him most for the enemies he has made," said General Edward S. Bragg in his seconding speech.[4]

The simplicity and steadfastness of the faith that sustained him throughout life is revealed in a letter written to his brother William, the Presbyterian minister. The note was penned as young Cleveland faced the awesome responsibilities of the governorship of New York: "Do you know that if Mother were alive I should feel so much safer? I have always thought her

[3] McElroy, Vol. I, p. 17.
[4] *Wisconsin State Journal,* July 10, 1884.

prayers had much to do with my success. I shall expect you to help me in that way." [5]

The New York governorship has often been called "the vestibule to the White House," and so it proved to be for Grover Cleveland. His refusal to play politics or indulge in spoils and patronage was not lost upon the public. In 1885 he was inaugurated president of the United States at the age of forty-eight.

Cleveland took the oath of office on a small Bible that was one of his most precious possessions. It had been given him by his mother in 1852 and was inscribed: "My son, Stephen Grover Cleveland from his loving Mother." This Bible was used at both of Cleveland's inaugurations, as twenty-second and twenty-fourth president.[6] The same Bible was used at the christening of two of his grandchildren.

While taking the oath, the president rested his hand on Psalm 112, which begins: "Praise ye the LORD. Blessed is the man that feareth the LORD, that delighteth greatly in his commandments."

Cleveland's first term was somewhat uneventful, except that it was marked by his unswerving adherence to the political principles that he deemed best for the nation.

In 1888, when Cleveland lost the campaign for a second term in the electoral college, he actually won a popular majority of 100,000 votes over Benjamin Harrison. In 1892, he became the only president ever elected to a second term nonconsecutively. This second victory rested largely on the strength of his reforming

---

[5] Nevins, p. 108.
[6] This Bible is now in the possession of Robert F. Cleveland, of Baltimore, Maryland.

zeal that he had displayed during his first term. Cleveland delivered his second inaugural address without a manuscript, a performance that impressed a great many people.

Shortly after his second inauguration, however, a financial panic swept the country, bringing with it one of the severest depressions that this nation had ever suffered—probably second only to that which began in 1929.

In 1894 a bitter labor war broke out at the Pullman Car Works in Chicago, whence it spread into every Midwestern railroad, bringing riots and bloodshed. President Cleveland used federal troops to break the strike within a week, in the face of strong opposition by Governor John P. Altgeld, of Illinois.

A third episode evoked worldwide interest. President Cleveland sought to apply the Monroe Doctrine successfully against Britain in a dispute between that country and Venezuela. The issue was finally arbitrated.

After his second Administration Cleveland retired to a quiet home in Princeton, New Jersey. He received many honors and nationally important appointments and has ever since been regarded as a model of fairness, honesty, and probity in the service of his country. He died on June 24, 1908, mourned by the American people. His last words were: "I have tried so hard to do right."

BENJAMIN HARRISON

BENJAMIN HARRISON

[1833–1901]

IF EVER A CANDIDATE FOR THE PRESIDENCY OF THE UNITED States appeared with shining credentials, the man was Benjamin Harrison. His great-grandfather, Benjamin, signed the Declaration of Independence and was three times governor of Virginia. His grandfather, William Henry Harrison, a renowned war hero known popularly as "Tippecanoe" for his most celebrated victory, became the ninth president of the United States. His father, John Scott Harrison, was a congressman in the House of Representatives, 1853–1857. Even Benjamin's education pointed in the direction of politics since his major interests at Miami University, Oxford, Ohio, were political science and history.

Yet Harrison was not the kind of man who leans heavily on his forebears and trades on the eminence they achieved. When on one occasion he was introduced as the grandson of President Harrison he replied: "I want it understood that I am the grandson of nobody. I believe that every man should stand on his own merits."

Benjamin Harrison was born at North Bend, Ohio,

August 20, 1833. He spent his youth working on his father's farm, which lay near the junction of the Big Miami and Ohio Rivers. His early schooling was under the direction of private tutors, who must have been able teachers because after three years at the Farmer's College near Cincinnati he was graduated from Miami University at the early age of eighteen. Immediately after graduation in 1852 he started the study of law and two years later was admitted to the Ohio bar.

It was during this period that Benjamin was perplexed by the question of vocation—specifically whether or not he should study for the ministry. Several able youths who afterward became American presidents had wrestled with the same question. This issue must have become quite insistent for two reasons: first, while he was a student in his teens at Miami University he had made a Christian decision during a revival, and second, because he had fallen very much in love with young Carrie Scott, the daughter of a Presbyterian minister, and married her. Incidentally, four other American presidents married daughters of ministers.

In the case of young Benjamin Harrison, however, as already noted he decided for the law, not unlikely with the presidency as a distant possibility. So at the age of twenty-one he and his young bride moved from Ohio to Indiana, with Indianapolis, at that time a town of 16,000 inhabitants, their future home.

Benjamin Harrison's career, both legal and political, was interrupted by the Civil War. He enlisted as a colonel taking an infantry regiment that he had recruited with him into the Northern forces. He fought in several engagements, the most important being the Atlantic campaign under General William T. Sherman, and was rewarded by promotion to brevet rank of brigadier general. The dispatches spoke of Harrison's "ability, manifest energy and gallantry"—high praise indeed.

Back in civil life, in 1872 and 1876 he made two attempts to reach the governorship of Indiana. He failed in both efforts. However, in 1881 he was elected to the United States Senate. After seven more years of marking time he went to the Chicago Republican Convention as "Indiana's favorite son," was nominated, and later elected president of the United States, defeating Cleveland, who received 168 electoral votes to Harrison's 233. The contest had turned on protection versus free trade. Harrison's election was a triumph for protection. The two rival candidates would meet again in 1892 with the results reversed.

President Harrison's Administration was not particularly distinguished but, as was true of his efforts in other areas, was a job well done. The results he achieved in the international field, such as the first international conference of American states, the settlement of controversies with Chile and Great Britain, were more significant than any accomplishments in the domestic arena.

As to courage and integrity in public life, and especially opposition to corrupt politicians, Harrison's Administration was of the quality of Hayes's, Garfield's, and Cleveland's. He earned the hatred and opposition of advocates of patronage and the spoils system but the respect of all men who love justice and probity.

Benjamin Harrison's church life was most active. He was elected a deacon and later an elder of the Presbyterian Church. He taught in the Sunday school, regularly attended services, organized Bible classes in the church and in the Y.M.C.A., and occasionally addressed the General Assembly of the Presbyterian Church U.S.A.

When Harrison's son, Russell, found himself in financial distress because of unwise speculation, his father did not immediately rush to his aid with monetary assistance, but instead gave him some salutary advice: "There is nothing for you except to meet your difficulties bravely and squarely. . . . Do not let any pressure of seeming necessity draw you one inch away from the line of honor and duty. . . . Prayer steadies one when he is walking in slippery places."[1]

Benjamin Harrison, universally recognized as a stalwart Christian, died on March 13, 1901. He was sixty-seven years of age.

---

[1] Fuller and Green, *God in the White House,* p. 155.

WILLIAM McKINLEY

WILLIAM McKINLEY

[1843–1901]

THE PREPARATION OF WILLIAM MCKINLEY FOR THE CHAL-
lenging and exacting post of president of the United
States, as with many another great man, began long
before his birth. He came from rugged Scotch-Irish
stock. To this was added the strength and stability of
Puritan character. His ancestors in America were known
as founders; that is, they made pig iron in blast fur-
naces, a trade that called for physical strength and
not a little skill. William McKinley, Sr., the father of
the future president, took up the founder's trade at
the age of sixteen. This meant a deficient schooling,
but he vowed that his children would not suffer the
same disadvantage.

William, Jr., the seventh child of the family, was
born in Niles, Ohio, January 29, 1843. Consequently,
some of the older children of the family had a hand
in his upbringing. Finding the facilities for schooling
at Niles somewhat below par, the McKinley family
moved to Poland, not far from Youngstown, Ohio. After
completing his studies there, William went to Allegheny
College, Meadville, Pennsylvania.

At seventeen William McKinley enlisted as a private in the Civil War. Fortunately for him he served under Rutherford B. Hayes, who was also destined to become president of the United States. Having received several promotions in rank and engaging in several battles, McKinley was finally mustered out with the brevet rank of major.

William, to the disappointment of his mother, who had hoped he would become a minister, settled for the practice of law and politics, making a permanent home in Canton, Ohio. There he married Ida Saxton, the daughter of an influential banker. The marriage was a deeply affectionate one, but a fearful blight fell on the home. First, both of their children died in infancy and perhaps even more tragic, Ida became a lifelong invalid from epilepsy with embarrassing seizures liable to happen at any time or place. For the rest of their married life Ida was the constant object of William's tenderest solicitude.

These calamities were accepted by the McKinleys with Christian serenity and did not prevent their active participation in the work of the First Methodist Church. Like President Benjamin Harrison, McKinley taught in the Sunday school, presided as superintendent, provided leadership for the Y.M.C.A., and organized temperance societies.

William McKinley from his childhood was religiously minded. When a revival was held at Poland, he at the age of ten marched up to the front of the church with manly dignity to become a member on probation.[1] Several years later he was received into full membership of the Methodist Church. From this time forward

---

[1] Charles S. Olcott, *The Life of William McKinley*, Vol. I, p. 19.

to the day of his death William McKinley never swerved from the high allegiance he had pledged to the One whom he had accepted as Lord and Master.

Now, in the postwar period, McKinley began to devote his tremendous energies to his law practice and to his advancement politically. In 1876 he was elected to the House of Representatives. Defying organized gerrymandering, he was elected six additional times, attracting the attention and backing of President Rutherford B. Hayes. McKinley had now become a national figure and as such gained the powerful support of Mark Hanna, a politically powerful and very wealthy banker.

Surprisingly, McKinley, in the face of formidable opposition, was elected governor of Ohio in 1891, and this strategic post was to be his sounding board for two terms beginning in 1892. Now the White House loomed up conspicuously on the horizon.

Suddenly the McKinleys were struck a staggering blow. As an act of friendship McKinley had signed a number of large notes for a friend. When the friend's business failed, McKinley was faced with the loss of every cent he owned. Immediately Mrs. McKinley, in spite of the disapproval of her attorney, gave her husband the entire estate she had received from her father. In reply to demurring friends she said: "My husband has done everything for me all my life. Do you mean to deny me the privilege of doing what I please with my own property to help him now?" [2] Finally a group of devoted friends whose names he never did know, underwrote the greater part of the debt for McKinley.

In the face of a campaign of defamation against him

[2] *Ibid.,* Vol. II, pp. 290–291.

McKinley won the Republican nomination in 1896 and was elected president by 271 electoral votes to 176 for William Jennings Bryan.

In his first inaugural he kissed the open Bible at the passage, "Give me now wisdom and knowledge, that I may go out and come in before this people: for who can judge this thy people, that is so great?" (II Chron. 1:10.)

The McKinleys maintained their habit of church-going in Washington as they had done elsewhere. During their years in the capital they attended the Metropolitan Methodist Church. McKinley continued the practice adopted by Rutherford Hayes of holding a hymn sing on Sunday evenings at the White House. They sang such hymns as "There's a Wideness in God's Mercy" and "Jesus, Lover of My Soul."

The major events of his first term and that portion of the second before it ended in his death were closely related. The Spanish-American War brought such international problems as the independence of Cuba and the disposition of the Philippines. Puerto Rico was made a protectorate and Hawaii was annexed.

The climax of William McKinley's life was attained at the Pan-American Exposition in September, 1901, in Buffalo. On September 5, he sounded the notes of high statesmanship and prophetic solemnity. "God and man have linked the nations together. . . . The period of exclusiveness is past. . . . No nation can be indifferent to any other." His address concluded with these words: "Let us ever remember . . . that our real eminence lies in victories of peace, not those of war. . . . Our earnest prayer is that God will graciously vouchsafe prosperity, happiness and peace to all our neigh-

161

bors, and like blessings to all peoples and powers on earth." [3] Little wonder his words were greeted with a thunderous ovation.

On September 6 a long receiving line waited at the Exposition Temple of Music. Thousands wanted to shake hands with the well-loved president. In the line was an innocent-looking young man with a bandaged hand. When he reached the point where the president stood, with scarcely a foot of space between them, as McKinley smiled and stretched out his hand to the youth, two shots rang out from a pistol concealed under the bandage. The president reeled and would have fallen had not a secret service detective caught him in his arms. "Am I shot?" was the president's question.

In the meantime secret service agents had leaped upon the youth whose name was Leon Czolgosz, a professed anarchist, and the crowd started beating him. President McKinley, seeing what was happening, said to an officer, "Don't let them hurt him."

His first thought had been for his beloved wife. As they were lifting him onto a stretcher he caught sight of his secretary, George B. Cortelyou, and said in an urgent whisper, "My wife—be careful, Cortelyou, how you tell her—oh, be careful." [4]

On the operating table McKinley said quietly to the surgeon, "I am in your hands." As the anesthetic was being administered the president's lips were moving and those about the table caught the words: "Thy kingdom come, thy will be done." Despite all that the medical service of the day could do, an infection was rapidly spreading. Eight days after the shooting the president

---

[3] *Ibid.*, pp. 311–312.
[4] *Ibid.*, pp. 315–318.

said: "It is useless, gentlemen. I think we ought to pray." His wife was sent for. In a few minutes he said: "Good-by, good-by, all. . . . It is God's way. His will, not ours, be done." The lips moved once more and the worn face became radiant as they heard him whisper the words of his best-loved hymn:

> "Nearer, my God, to Thee,
> Nearer to Thee!
> E'en though it be a cross . . ."

and then silence.[5]

Not since the death of Abraham Lincoln had the anguish of personal grief so penetrated every household in the nation. Now there were three martyred presidents to mourn—Lincoln, Garfield, and McKinley—noble, dedicated men who died for their country.

---

[5] *Ibid.*, pp. 324–327.

THEODORE ROOSEVELT

THEODORE ROOSEVELT

[1858–1919]

ROOSEVELT WAS THE ONLY UNITED STATES PRESIDENT TO be born in New York City. His birthplace was 28 East 20th Street and the date October 27, 1858. He was the second of four children. Six generations of his family had some identification with Manhattan. In the main the Roosevelt family prospered. They belonged to the upper class of New York society. Traditionally they shunned vulgar display, but stressed education and cultural development.

When Roosevelt was sixteen years of age he joined the Dutch Reformed Church, the same age at which William McKinley, under whom he was destined to serve as vice-president, had become a member of the Methodist Church. In Washington he and his family attended the Grace Reformed Church with commendable regularity. In his youth the family often worshiped in the Madison Square Presbyterian Church, which was conveniently located to their home. It is evident that neither Theodore nor his parents felt tied down to any one denomination. Both his mother and his second wife were Episcopalians. Theodore Roosevelt and his family attended the Episcopal Church in Oyster Bay, Long Island, reverting to the Dutch Reformed when in Washington.

As we might expect, Roosevelt had decided views on religion and the Bible. He believed and practiced a "muscular Christianity," a religion of confidence and action. One of his favorite texts was, "Be ye doers of the word, and not hearers only, deceiving your own selves." (James 1:22.)

Because of his delicate health Theodore received his early schooling by tutors. Consequently, he missed the rough-and-tumble of life with other boys. However, with set determination he worked daily to build up his physique. His knowledge of other lands and peoples was broadened by several visits to Europe. He was fortunate also that a French governess lived with the family, and the familiarity with the French language that young Theodore acquired in his boyhood was retained throughout his life.

He was sent to Harvard, was graduated in 1880 *magna cum laude*, and was elected Phi Beta Kappa. The same year he married Alice Hathaway Lee, of Boston.

Roosevelt was an omniverous reader and among the earliest presidents only Jefferson, John Quincy Adams, and perhaps Madison matched his passion for knowledge. He reveled in history and wrote intelligently on the military and naval history of the United States.

Roosevelt's first venture into politics resulted in three sessions at Albany, where he made his presence felt. He gave the reporters ample copy and was the acknowledged leader of a small but influential group who joined with him in fighting political corruption. Shortly thereafter came a three-year interval which Roosevelt spent in the Dakota Territory, where he lived the life of a ranchman and built his body into superb physical fitness. It was in this period too that he became a first-class horseman. He invested $50,000 of the patrimony he received on the death of his father in large tracts of land. The land investment did not pay off, but the health investment brought him lifelong dividends.

In 1886 Roosevelt returned to New York as a candidate in a mayoralty race which he lost. In the same year, his first wife having died two years earlier, he married Edith Kermit Carow, a friend of his childhood days. They made their home thereafter in Sagamore Hill, near Oyster Bay, Long Island.

President Benjamin Harrison, who was essentially a reformer, appointed Roosevelt a member of the United States Civil Service Commission in Washington, and for six years he fought the advocates of the spoils system. In 1895 he became president of the police board of New York City. Quickly he built up the morale of the force by substituting a system of appointment and promotion for merit and rooted out corrupt practices.

In 1898 he was elected governor of New York State, in which post he served for two years. His political foes within his own party now schemed to make him vice-president during McKinley's second term. In this way they could remove him from active politics. Roosevelt himself called the vice-presidency "taking the veil." John Adams described the vice-presidency as "the most insignificant office that ever the invention of man contrived or his imagination conceived." [1] Republican bosses led by Thomas C. Platt succeeded in their

---

[1] A letter from John Adams to his wife, Abigail, 1789.

scheme to put Roosevelt in that position. Little could they know what the end result would be!

On September 14, 1901, a few weeks short of his forty-third birthday and immediately following the death by assassination of President McKinley, Theodore Roosevelt was sworn in as president of the United States. He was the youngest man ever to take this high office, just as John Fitzgerald Kennedy, though older than Roosevelt, was the youngest man in United States history to be *elected* to the presidency.

The achievements of Theodore Roosevelt in the presidency were so numerous and far-reaching that, having regard to the limitations of space, we can do little more than indicate their range and nature: the curbing of trusts, monopolies, and holding companies; the right of the president to act as a representative of the people in the event of strikes and lockouts; important regulations regarding the operation of the railroads; pure food laws; the inspection of stockyards and packing houses; the prohibition of adulterated foods, medicines, and liquors; far-reaching laws for the conservation of forests and water power resources; appointment of a conservation commission to prepare an inventory, the first ever made in any nation, of all natural resources in the United States.

Similarly, in the international sphere he grappled with unresolved controversies with other nations and settled them in a spirit of frankness, boldness, and undeniable friendliness. He made the United States a nation of the first rank, admired, feared, its favor sought after, its citizenship respected in the remotest corner of the globe.[2]

[2] *Encyclopædia Britannica,* Vol. XIX, p. 537.

It has been said that Washington founded America and Lincoln preserved its unity. It may be added that Theodore Roosevelt revitalized and rejuvenated it. The vigor and abounding vitality of Roosevelt infected the whole nation with a new spirit of national pride and hopefulness. A new era had just come to birth with the beginning of a new century.

All that President Roosevelt said and did was undergirded by his faith in the overruling Providence of God. He knew the Bible well and continually refreshed his spirit by its message. The passage which he chose and on which he laid his hand when he was sworn into office at the first inaugural typifies his concept of religion: "He hath showed thee, O man, what is good; and what doth the LORD require of thee, but to do justly, and to love mercy, and to walk humbly with thy God?" (Micah 6:8.)

In counting the achievements of Theodore Roosevelt, we have made no mention up to this point of his faults. He had plenty of them and they were visible for all men to see. By and large they lay on the surface of his life. Highly gifted men, especially when they possess tremendous drive, can sometimes forget that most of their fellowmen are not similarly endowed and require on the part of their leaders sympathetic understanding and patience. Roosevelt lacked patience and oftentimes when he was opposed would call his adversaries harsh and contemptuous names.

Shakespeare makes a character in *Julius Caesar* say: "The evil that men do lives after them, The good is oft interred with their bones."

The reverse of this has been true of Theodore Roosevelt. Would that it could always be so!

Roosevelt had frequently remarked that death is, under all circumstances, a tragedy. Mercifully he was spared the knowledge of its approach, for he died in his sleep in his sixty-first year, January 6, 1919.

WILLIAM HOWARD TAFT

WILLIAM HOWARD TAFT

[1857–1930]

FREQUENTLY A CANDIDATE FOR THE PRESIDENCY OF THE United States has had forebears who, in one way or another, have been prominent in politics. This was true of William Howard Taft. His father, Alphonso, was attorney general in President Grant's cabinet. Later he was American minister to Austria and Russia. William Howard himself was salutatorian of his class at Yale College in 1878 and at Cincinnati Law School two years later.

Taft was employed in several inconspicuous legal positions until his most significant responsibility was given him by President William McKinley. It was the presidency of the Philippine Commission. The critical matter of the confiscation of large tracts of Roman Catholic property and payment for the same now came to the fore. In 1902, Taft went to Rome for an interview with Pope Leo XIII and the following year $7,-239,000 was paid to the pope for the land. This transaction was used against Taft when he was running for the presidency and he was called "a tool of Rome."

From 1904 to 1908 Taft was given a number of assignments in Cuba, Puerto Rico, the Philippines, and Japan.

In 1908 with the powerful backing of Theodore Roosevelt, William Howard Taft was elected president of the United States by a plurality of over 1,269,900 votes. He was defeated in his attempt to win a second term principally because Roosevelt split the Republican vote by making a third try for the presidency. Consequently, Woodrow Wilson, the Democratic nominee, was elected.

Taft has put little in writing that would indicate his personal religious thinking. The closest approach to such a revelation resulted from an invitation to accept the presidency of Yale University. To his brother, Henry Taft, who was pressing the invitation, he wrote that because of the tradition at Yale of always having a Congregational clergyman for president many of the alumni and supporters would be shocked to learn that the post had been given to one "who could not subscribe to the creed of the Orthodox Congregational Church of New England." He then explicitly states his denominational preference: "I am a Unitarian. I believe in God. I do not believe in the Divinity of Christ. . . . I am not however a scoffer at religion but on the contrary recognize, in the fullest manner, the elevating influence that it has had and always will have in the history of mankind." [1]

Part of this statement by Taft before he became president is in striking contrast to a signed and dated declaration by President McKinley two years after he had taken office: "My belief embraces the Divinity of

---

[1] Letter to Taft's brother, January, 1899.

Christ and a recognition of Christianity as the mightiest factor in the world's civilization." [2]

In his youth Taft attended a Unitarian Sunday school and read the Bible with some degree of regularity. When the matter of his Unitarian background was raised as a campaign issue he said: "If the American electorate is so narrow as not to elect a Unitarian, well and good. I can stand it."

A further indication of William Howard Taft's thinking with respect to the Christian faith is given in words excerpted from a public address: "The spirit of Christianity is pure democracy. It is the equality of man before God—the equality of man before the law, which is, as I understand it, the most God-like manifestation that man has been able to make." [3] One does not find in these words any strong commitment to traditional Christianity.

It may be regarded as evidence of a devotional spirit in President Taft's home that his son Charles became an avowed Christian, uniting with the Episcopal Church and later in life was elected president of the Federal Council of the Churches of Christ in America. Among his published books is one entitled *Why I Am for the Church*.

On June 30, 1921, William Howard Taft was appointed chief justice of the Supreme Court by President Warren G. Harding. At last he had been given a position of high responsibility where his legal abilities could find true expression.

It was William Howard Taft's misfortune to reach the presidency immediately following that born leader

---

[2] A personal memo dated May 26, 1899.
[3] Conference of Laymen's Missionary Movement, New York, 1908.

of men, Theodore Roosevelt. Taft was a comparatively good administrator, though many of his recommendations never came to fruition, chiefly because he could not inspire men to follow him. He was emphatically not a leader.

After bad health, due chiefly to heart disease, forced his retirement from the bench, he died in Washington on March 8, 1930.

WOODROW WILSON

WOODROW WILSON

[1856–1924]

ON SUNDAY MORNING A LARGE CONGREGATION WAS GATH-
ered in the First Presbyterian Church, Augusta, Georgia. At the announcement period a tall, well-built minister looked down at his people and said: "At this very
moment a battle is being fought in Virginia and our
Confederate forces are in grave need of ammunition.
This congregation must do its duty. Immediately at
the close of these services the ladies will repair to the
munitions factory to help with the cartridges. You will
now rise and sing the Doxology and be dismissed."

Sitting in front of the preacher was a five-year-old
fair-haired lad who gazed at the man in the pulpit with
love and pride. He was the minister's son. That boy
was destined one day to be the president of the United
States.

Woodrow Wilson was born in Staunton, Virginia, on
December 28, 1856. His father was Joseph Ruggles
Wilson, a thoroughly educated and eloquent Presbyterian minister. When young Woodrow was less than a
year old his father received a call to the First Pres-

byterian Church of Augusta, Georgia. It was a decided promotion since Augusta was a prosperous town of more than 12,000 inhabitants. The Wilsons remained there for some twelve years. Even though Rev. Ruggles Wilson was born in Ohio, when the Civil War split the nation asunder his sympathies were entirely with the South. Young Woodrow therefore lived through the horrors of the war, seeing it only from the Southern viewpoint. Half a century later Wilson reported his earliest recollection. He heard a passerby shout excitedly that Lincoln had won the election and war was coming. He asked his father what this meant.[1]

Young Woodrow saw and felt at first hand the ravages of the war and even greater sufferings of the people during the reconstruction period. The churchyard had been a prison camp for Northern soldiers. The church itself was a hospital filled with the dead and dying. These recollections must have been plowed and harrowed into his young, sensitive, and retentive mind. The remembrance of these years might well have been a factor in his prolonged reluctance, when he was president, to plunge the United States into what was swiftly becoming a world war.

Without accepting the psychological inferences and conclusions drawn from Woodrow Wilson's life and his relations with his father by Freud and Bullitt, students of biography readily admit that there was an abnormally close relationship between father and son. Ray Stannard Baker, Wilson's official biographer who had all the Wilson family papers, says that Woodrow never

---

[1] Sigmund Freud and William C. Bullitt, *Thomas Woodrow Wilson: A Psychological Study,* p. 6.

made an important decision in his life, of any kind, up to the age of forty, without consulting his father.[2]

The influence of his father remained with him always. All his life he prayed on his knees morning and evening. Every day he read the Bible. He wore out two or three Bibles in the course of his life. He said grace before every meal. He believed that through prayer he was specifically guided of God.[3]

After a brief and unsatisfactory experience at Davidson College, North Carolina, Wilson entered Princeton University in 1875. There he was especially active in debating and literary circles. After graduation from Princeton he studied law at the University of Virginia and secured a Ph.D. at Johns Hopkins in Baltimore.

About this time he married Ellen Louise Axson and began the literary career that was climaxed by his becoming first a professor and then president of Princeton University. His efforts to democratize and reform this institution aroused much opposition and largely failed, but by now his speeches and published articles on political questions brought him to the attention of the politicians. He was given the Democratic nomination for the governorship of New Jersey and won the election. While in this office he carried through dynamic programs of reform in the face of strong opposition of the machine politicians. The Corrupt Practices Act was so successful that Wilson now was attracting nationwide attention.

On July 2, 1912, he was nominated by the Democratic Party as their candidate for the presidency and

---

[2] Ray Stannard Baker and William E. Dodd (eds.), *The Public Papers.*
[3] Freud and Bullitt, p. 7.

in November of the same year was elected president of the United States.

Woodrow Wilson lost no time in bringing to pass the major items he had stressed in his campaign. Some of his legislative achievements were: more flexible tariff laws, a federal income tax, child labor bill, currency reform, workmen's compensation, antitrust laws, women's suffrage, and the right of labor to strike.

Wilson's foreign policy is not easy to define, but various moves of a military and naval nature made under his direction helped to establish an assured place for the United States among the great powers of the world.

The Great War of 1914–1918 now overshadowed all other issues and the president was constantly occupied with the task of protecting the rights of the United States as a neutral nation. First, there were clashes with Britain over the blockade of German ports. This issue soon took a decidedly secondary role to the gradually extending threat against neutral shipping by German submarines. After the sinking of the *Lusitania* with the loss of over 1,000 persons, including 128 Americans, President Wilson's mind was firmly and finally made up: indiscriminate sinking of ships without warning must cease.

Having been returned to power by a small majority in November, 1916, President Wilson sought to institute peace negotiations with the belligerent. In answer came the German renewal of unrestricted submarine warfare. This and the publishing of the notorious Zimmermann telegram greatly inflamed American public opinion. (In 1916, the German secretary of state, Arthur Zimmermann, sent a highly secret telegram to

183

Mexico inviting her to join an alliance against the United States. In return, Mexico was to be given New Mexico, Texas, and Arizona. The telegram also suggested that Mexico should sound out Japan about joining the alliance. It was intercepted by the British and transmitted to President Wilson on March 1, 1917. Wilson immediately publicized it in the U.S.A.) After exasperating delays President Wilson finally asked for a declaration of a state of war. The necessary resolutions were passed in both the Senate and the House of Representatives with overwhelming majorities.

President Wilson swiftly mobilized the army and the nation for war. He used with great effectiveness as a moral weapon proclamations of the noble intentions of the Allies to bring justice and freedom to all peoples. These declarations penetrated into Germany and gradually weakened that nation's will to fight and hastened her surrender.

The debates and intrigues that took place at the Versailles Peace Conference are now common knowledge. What is not so fully known is that there is every reason to believe that Congress would have ratified the League of Nations proposal had Wilson been willing to negotiate Article X on collective security to which great objection was made. On the contrary, he advised his followers not to vote for the resolution with a reservation on Article X. Twenty-three of them abstained. Consequently, the United States was "kept out of the League of Nations" by the man who had done more than any other to create it.[4] We now know that the League of Nations was a dangerously imperfect instru-

---

[4] *Encyclopædia Britannica,* Vol. XXIII, p. 642.

ment for promoting peace, for it had in it the seeds of World War II.

Defeated, heartbroken, crippled in body, clouded in mind, embittered in spirit, Woodrow Wilson, the greatest idealist of his time, died on February 3, 1924.

"I am content to leave my reputation to the verdict of history," Wilson once said. There is good reason to believe that history's verdict will be more just and more kind than that of his contemporaries. We have only to reflect that the more equitable peace that was effected by the Allies in 1945, though still a long way from perfection, was based to a considerable degree on the principles that Woodrow Wilson laid down in 1919.

What Robert Burns said of his father could be said with equal truth of Woodrow Wilson: "E'en his failings leaned to virtue's side." [5]

His faults were not those of evil purpose or low ideals but faults of temperament: an excess of self-confidence and self-reliance, an unwillingness to change his mind once he had made a decision, an assurance of his own rightness.

Dr. Henry Van Dyke, who knew him intimately both in Princeton and Washington, said, "Deep down in his soul was a great idealism—a high sense of honor—a genuineness—an unselfishness that would sacrifice all for an ideal." [6]

When history has finally rendered its verdict, we believe that Woodrow Wilson, like Abraham Lincoln, vilified and condemned, will be accorded a place with the greatest statesmen and patriots of this nation.

---

[5] Epitaph on his father's tomb, Alloway, Scotland.
[6] Harold Garnet Black, *The True Woodrow Wilson, Crusader for Democracy*, p. 255.

WARREN G. HARDING

Twenty-ninth President
1921–1923

WARREN G. HARDING

[1865–1923]

"WARREN G. HARDING HAS BEEN UNIVERSALLY REGARDED as the worst president the country has, up to this time, ever had."[1] Such is the verdict of Prof. John A. Garraty, of Columbia University. The questions have been asked repeatedly: How could such a deplorable event happen despite the safeguards of American democracy? Why did not the people become aware of the moral letdown that was in the making?

Edmund Fuller and David Green, biographers of Harding, answered such queries in these words: "That was precisely what the American people unconsciously wanted, a relief from both the tensions of war and the stern school-masterish President who had so long invoked their consciences and talked to them in moral tones."[2]

One is reminded of Aristides of Athens. Because this noble Athenian had cleansed the capital city of flagrant corruption and made justice available to all, the com-

---

[1] John A. Garraty, professor of history at Columbia University and the author of several books in *The New York Times Book Review*, Nov. 24, 1968.
[2] Fuller and Green, *God in the White House*, p. 184.

mon people admired him and gave him the surname "the Just." But after the battles were over and the victory was won they began to weary of Aristides and plotted his exile. On the day when the vote was being taken, in the public square, on his ostracism Aristides himself was present. He was approached by an illiterate fellow who, not recognizing the great Athenian, asked him to write the name of Aristides on the piece of pottery that was his ballot. Surprised, he asked the man if Aristides had ever done him wrong. "Not at all," said he, "neither do I know the man but I am tired of hearing him everywhere called 'the Just.'" Woodrow Wilson was the American Aristides.[3]

Warren Gamaliel Harding was born in Corsica, Ohio, on November 2, 1865. He was the son of G. T. Harding, a farmer who later became a doctor. His mother was a Dickerson. He was educated in a public school and Ohio Central College. He taught school, read law, and got a job on a newspaper. He advanced himself to editor and owner of the *Marion Star*, a four-page weekly for which he and a partner paid three hundred dollars. Harding took over the paper and built it into a successful small-town daily.

At the age of twenty-six he married Florence Kling, a competent businesswoman who was a divorcee and five years his senior. She was a large woman with a somewhat stern and formidable appearance which did not invite a closer acquaintance. Her coldness has been advanced by some of Harding's friends as an excuse for his amours.

Warren Harding was tall, good-looking, of command-

---

[3] Charles W. Eliot (ed.), *Plutarch's Lives* (Harvard Classics), Vol. XII, p. 88.

ing presence, and possessed an excellent speaking voice. He was a member of practically all the clubs and orders of Marion. He was decidedly popular with men. The ladies too found him attractive. With all these qualities and, for extra measure, owner and editor of a newspaper, it is not surprising that he should have come to the attention of the politicians. His climb to the highest office in the nation was rapid: two terms, 1900–1904, in the Ohio senate, 1904–1906 lieutenant governor of Ohio, 1914 nominated for the United States Senate, and elected for the term 1915–1921. At the Republican National Convention in 1920 he was at an early stage given scant consideration. On the first ballot he received only 65½ votes. It was not until the tenth ballot that he secured the nomination with 692½ votes.

Harding made no attempt to "go on the stump" but conducted a "front porch" campaign from his home. Quite indefinite as to what his program would be, he denounced the Wilson Administration and especially the excessive power of the executive. His goal would be "normal conditions," political and industrial.

The result was never in doubt. The popular vote for Harding was 16,152,000 with 9,147,000 for his Democratic opponent, James M. Cox, the greatest majority ever given to a president in a hundred years. The electoral vote was Harding 404 and Cox 127. The nation was set on a change of rulers and the popular feeling against President Wilson was running very strong.

At least three members of Harding's Cabinet met with instant and widespread approval. Charles Evans Hughes, secretary of state, Herbert C. Hoover, secretary of commerce, and Andrew W. Mellon, secretary of the treasury. No slightest taint of corruption touched segments of the Administration under the control of these and certain other able and honorable men. Of others, including Harry M. Daugherty, attorney general, and Albert B. Fall, secretary of the interior, little good can be said. It was not until after the sudden death of Harding that the oil leases, the Veterans Bureau, and other scandals leaped to light. When the law had taken its course, five of those found guilty went to prison. There were three suicides and many broken men.

After the publication of *The President's Daughter*, the material for which was supplied by attractive and lively Nan Britton, the president's involvement in moral scandals became known. It was all a terrible shock to Harding's many hero-worshipers. William Allen White, famous newspaper editor, wrote to Brant Whitlock: "God. What a story! The story of Babylon is a Sunday School story compared with the story of Washington from June 1919 to July 1923." [4]

The one really memorable achievement of Harding's Administration was the Washington Conference on Naval Limitation, 1921. It was attended by representatives of all the great naval powers as well as a few from smaller nations. Secretary of State Hughes presided. Bold and far-reaching proposals were made, some of which later bore fruit. But it is doubtful whether President Harding contributed in any substantial way to the conference.

President Harding collapsed during a speech in Seattle. When he arrived in San Francisco his illness was diagnosed as a heart attack with complications of pneumonia. He died suddenly on August 2, 1923. Nearly

[4] Quoted in Andrew Sinclair, *The Available Man*, p. 297.

eight years after President Harding's death all the political greats met at the dedication of the Harding tomb in Marion, Ohio. The address was to be given by President Hoover. There was tense uneasiness as to what the president would say. He hit out and hit hard: "Here was a man whose soul was seared by a great disillusionment. We saw him gradually weaken, not only from physical exhaustion, but also from mental anxiety. Warren Harding had a dim realization that he had been betrayed by a few of the men whom he had believed were his devoted friends. That was the tragedy of the life of Warren Harding."[5]

We know little or nothing of the inner commitments of Warren Harding in the matter of religion. Outwardly he manifested the appropriate deference toward the institution of religion which in this nation is expected of men in high public office. His mother was a devoted member of the Seventh-Day Adventist Church, but Warren Harding did not join any church until after he had become an influential citizen of Marion. Then he became a member and later a trustee of the Baptist Church. This relationship would become of increasing importance to him as he advanced in political life. After his election a friend wished him Godspeed. He replied: "Yes. God help me, for I shall need it."

His scandal-ridden term of office made his words prophetic.

---

[5] Samuel Hopkins Adams, *The Incredible Era,* p. 441.

CALVIN COOLIDGE

CALVIN COOLIDGE

[1872–1933]

JOHN ADAMS IN THE COMPANY OF A FRIEND WALKED INTO a museum where two busts, one of Washington and the other of himself, were on display. Adams, with his cane, pointed at the typically compressed lips of Washington and said, "That fellow knew how to keep his mouth shut." Then, tapping his own bust with his cane he added, "And this damn fool didn't!"

Whatever may have been characteristic of Adams, it was certainly true of Calvin Coolidge that he "knew how to keep his mouth shut." Coolidge was never criticized for loquacity.

The American people always enjoy jokes that embody some trait of personality in their presidents and a host of stories have been told on Coolidge's taciturnity. His brevity of words on August 2, 1927, is a case in point. "I do not choose to run for President in 1928." Mr. Coolidge doubtless had many a chuckle at the expense of the politicians and newspapermen who dissected and analyzed this phrase over and over again in an attempt to find a hidden meaning in the words.

Calvin Coolidge was unmistakably a New Englander

and was descended from several generations of farmers and shopkeepers. All of them lived unostentatiously with enough of the world's goods to keep their families in reasonable comfort. Young Calvin used to listen with interest to the discussions carried on in his father's store on matters of local, national, and even international concern. Early in this century these cracker-barrel debates were nightly occurrences in his community.

Calvin's schooling began in Plymouth, Vermont, where he was born on July 4, 1872. His parents were John Calvin Coolidge and Victoria J. Moor Coolidge. They were firm believers in a good education for their children. Consequently, after attending two academies, Calvin entered Amherst College in 1891. He promptly demonstrated his capacity for hard work, though this was rarely evidenced by high grades, yet he was chosen Grove Orator for the class commencement exercises of 1895.

On graduation he plunged at once into the study of law in Northampton with some practical experience in local politics. For two terms he served as mayor of Northampton, then was elected to the state senate. He won repeated promotion: president of the senate, lieutenant governor of Massachusetts (three terms), and governor of Massachusetts in 1919 and 1920. Each election result showed increasing majorities. All this was achieved without ostentation or flashy advertising. He said, "We need more of the office desk and less of the show window in politics." And that exactly is what he gave the electorate.

As governor of Massachusetts he demonstrated his capacity as an administrator. This alone would not have given him national prominence had it not been for his proved ability in settling the strike of the Boston policemen. The strike resulted from the police commissioner's refusal to permit affiliation with the American Federation of Labor. On September 9, 1919, three fourths of the policemen walked off their posts. Disorder and riots spread throughout Boston.

Coolidge called out the entire National Guard and personally took charge of the police department. The strike was broken and order restored. Striking policemen were not reinstated. In concise and crystal-clear phrases Coolidge stated why: "There is no right to strike against the public safety by anybody, anywhere, anytime." The entire nation was impressed by his leadership, and at the next national Republican Convention he was swept into nomination as vice-president on the first ballot.

In the early morning of August 3, 1923, while at his father's home in Plymouth, he learned of the death of President Warren Harding. The genuineness of Coolidge's religious faith is seen in the fact that being informed of the president's death, he paused to pray before dressing.

When a clamor arose for a clean sweep of accused officeholders of the Harding regime, in strong, terse phrases Coolidge demonstrated his command of the situation. He declared that he would not sacrifice an innocent man or maintain in office an unfit one.

When the 1924 conventions and federal election came along he calmly awaited the result. It was a sweeping victory which kept him firmly in office.

Neither on the international nor on the domestic front were any dramatic programs put through by Coolidge. More importantly he ensured that the last vestiges of the Harding corruption were cleaned out and the business of the country was put on a stable and trustworthy basis. Economic prosperity everywhere evident throughout the country produced an atmosphere of buoyancy and hopefulness.

Periodically he addressed the nation somewhat after the fashion later employed so effectively by Franklin Delano Roosevelt. His voice was reassuring and he made his comments with such clarity that these talks drew president and people closer together. There was consequently great disappointment when he stated unequivocally that he would not run for office again.

That Calvin Coolidge was a spiritually-minded man was beyond dispute. As in other New England centers most families attended Congregational churches. Young Calvin was taught the Bible and respect for his parents both in the Sunday school and in his own home. He speaks in his autobiography of his great love for his mother. She had long been an invalid but, as is always the case, he was unprepared for her death. He was twelve years old and his mother thirty-nine when she died. "The greatest grief that can come to a boy came to me. Life was never to seem the same again." One precious memory would never be erased: the children knelt that sad day at the mother's bedside and received her blessing.

President Coolidge tells how, as a boy, during his grandfather's illness, he used to read at his frequent request from the Gospel of John, the first chapter. Then he adds: "On taking the oath as President I placed my hand on that book of the Bible in memory of my first reading of it." [1] Later, he made his profession of faith,

[1] *The Autobiography of Calvin Coolidge*, p. 13.

through partaking of the Communion, and so became a member of the Congregational Church of Washington, D.C.

It has sometimes been suggested that President Coolidge was an austere and unemotional man. Anyone who reads thoughtfully his autobiography will discover that he was a man of unusually deep feelings. For instance, he tells how his sixteen-year-old son developed blood poisoning from a blister on his foot as he played tennis on the south lawn of the White House. "In his suffering he was asking me to make him well. I could not. When he went the power and the glory of the presidency went with him." [2]

Calvin Coolidge's concept of the presidency motivated his life during his entire time in office. He declared that anyone who has carried this awesome responsibility "comes to realize, with an increasing sense of humility, that he is but an instrument in the hands of God." [3]

[2] *Ibid.*, p. 190.
[3] *Ibid.*

HERBERT C. HOOVER

HERBERT C. HOOVER

[1874–1964]

UNTIL THE INAUGURATION OF RICHARD M. NIXON, HERBERT Hoover was the only representative of the Society of Friends to become president of the United States. Both of Hoover's parents were Friends, or Quakers, as they are more popularly called. The term "Quaker" was first given by Justice Bennet in 1650 as a nickname for George Fox because the latter had bid the justice "to tremble at the Word of the Lord." [1] The term "Friends," which Fox applied to this religious movement, he took from the saying of Jesus: "Ye are my friends, if ye do whatsoever I command you." (John 15:14.)

The Quaker faith powerfully influenced the lives of many people in Britain and America and was professed by men and women from all segments of society, sometimes in the face of severe persecution. Its testimony against war, slavery, racial segregation, alcohol, gambling, and poverty in England and America brought positive results in human reformation. An Anglican prelate, the celebrated William Ralph Inge, dean of

---

[1] F. L. Cross (ed.), *The Oxford Dictionary of the Christian Church,* p. 1130.

St. Paul's Cathedral, London, wrote: "The Quakers of all Christian bodies have remained nearest to the teaching and example of Christ." [2] On this side of the Atlantic, Harvard's philosopher William James said: "The Quaker religion which George Fox founded is something which it is impossible to overpraise. In a day of shams it was a religion of veracity rooted in spiritual inwardness and a return to something more like the original gospel truth." [3]

Herbert Hoover's whole life was rooted and grounded in the faith so zealously taught him by his Quaker parents in his tenderest and most impressionable years. This is the clue to an understanding of a complex and extraordinary man.

Hoover himself gives us an intimate picture of how thoroughgoing was his religious training: "Individual Bible-reading was a part of the Quaker concept of education—and before I had left Iowa I had read the Bible in daily stints from cover to cover. Religious training among the Quakers in fact begins almost before birth. Even the babies were present at the invariable family prayers and Bible-reading every morning. They were taken to meeting every Sunday since obviously there was no other place in which to park them. Their cries and hushings thereof were often the only relief from the long silences of Quaker worship." [4]

Herbert Clark Hoover was born on August 10, 1874, in West Branch, Iowa. His birthplace was a tiny one-story, three-room cottage. Herbert's father, Jesse Clark Hoover, was a blacksmith turned farm implements

[2] Leo Rosten (ed.), *The Religions of America.*
[3] *Ibid.*
[4] Herbert Hoover, *Memoirs,* Vol. I, p. 8.

dealer. Herbert was only six years old when his father died. Even at that tender age he grasped something of the privations his mother, Hulda Hoover, with three small children had to undergo. She took in sewing to help keep food in the family larder. Later he learned that she had actually received one thousand dollars from her husband's insurance but kept it intact for the children's education. Two years after his father's death his mother also died. He was sent to the home of an uncle, Henry John Minthorn, a country doctor in Oregon. While he was doing odd jobs as office boy and general helper providentially he met an engineer who turned his thoughts toward a college education.

Hoover entered Stanford University as a member of the freshman class, working his way to an A.B. degree by operating a laundry, typing, and running a newspaper route.

After graduation he worked in California and Australia. Always he continued studying to increase his knowledge and skill. Later he went to China to the position of chief engineer of the Chinese Bureau of Mines. About this time he married Lou Henry, a Stanford graduate in geology. A member of the Episcopal Church, she now became a devout Quaker.

The geographic range of his employment reads like a travel brochure: Russia, China, India, Australia, New Zealand, South Africa, Canada, Great Britain, Belgium, as well as many parts of the United States. He was soon a man of wealth.

With the advent of World War I, Herbert Hoover began his prodigious and forever memorable labors on behalf of the destitute people of Belgium. Under his direction almost one billion dollars was spent on this noble effort. In the closing months of World War I and for a year thereafter Hoover furnished more than eighteen million tons of food to the Allies and famine-stricken areas of Europe. Eventually he established a relief program for ten million homeless and destitute children. Additional similar programs for European children brought financial support of over one quarter of a billion dollars.

After Calvin Coolidge had issued his cryptic statement declining to run again it was not surprising that the eyes of tens of thousands turned to Herbert Hoover. It is doubtful if any other president in this nation's history approached this office more thoroughly equipped than he to deal with complex problems, national and international. He was nominated at the Republican National Convention of 1928 and elected president with four and one half million votes more than were received by Calvin Coolidge in 1924.

Despite Mr. Hoover's record as a skilled administrator the economic depression of 1929 turned the American people against him. He left the presidency a rejected man, but sustained by the faith that had brought past generations of his people through untold troubles, he never lost his moral strength, his courage, or his hope. He lived to see the shadows lifted and himself esteemed, valued, and beloved by a grateful nation.

FRANKLIN D. ROOSEVELT

FRANKLIN D. ROOSEVELT

[1882–1945]

FRANKLIN DELANO ROOSEVELT, SO FAR AS WORLDLY GOODS are concerned, was a long sea mile removed from the "log cabin" presidents of earlier years. His father, James Roosevelt, was a wealthy landowner and railway executive. His mother, Sarah Delano Roosevelt, came from a family of merchants and shippers of considerable means. He was born at Hyde Park, New York, January 30, 1882.

The financial independence of his family gave him, from his earliest years, every opportunity for acquiring a first-class education. European travel for him began at the age of three and, like Theodore Roosevelt, he early mastered conversational French, to which he added German. From Groton School he went on to Harvard (1900), completing his studies at Columbia Law School in 1904.

Franklin Roosevelt married his distant cousin Anna Eleanor Roosevelt. The wedding was attended by the bride's uncle, President Theodore Roosevelt. There were frequent informal meetings of Franklin and Eleanor with President Theodore Roosevelt both in the White House and at Oyster Bay. Unquestionably Franklin's interest in politics was immensely stimulated by these talks with the president.

Franklin Delano Roosevelt lost no time in starting to climb the political ladder. Here are some of the successive stages in his progress: New York state senator, assistant secretary of the Navy (under President Wilson). Then followed a hiatus of four years from August, 1921, to 1924, when Roosevelt was stricken with infantile paralysis. With undiscourageable grit and determination he fought his physical impairments and recovered to the extent that by 1928 he had become governor of New York State, continuing in that office till 1932. That fall he was elected president, defeating Herbert Hoover and carrying all but six states. He won a second term in 1936 and was elected for a third term—a new departure in American history, and now prohibited by the recent twenty-second amendment to the Constitution. In 1944 he was elected for a fourth term.

We must leave to history a final appraisal of Roosevelt's economic and social programs, but there is no gainsaying the fact that his forceful, dynamic personality, which everyone knew had carried him through a disabling illness, had a profoundly stimulating effect on the nation's morale. Never, except perhaps in wartime, had the Congress passed so many far-reaching economic and social programs. The keynote of his first inaugural address was "the only thing we have to fear is fear itself." These words, quoted and requoted from the Atlantic to the Pacific, helped to vanquish the spirit of pessimism and unreasoning panic. (It has seldom been noted that this epigram in a slightly altered form is found in Thoreau's *Journal:* "Nothing is so much to be feared as fear.")

In 1939 the president valiantly sought to keep the country out of the war while maintaining a modified neutrality which leaned toward the Allies in such matters as lend-lease of fifty American destroyers and other matériel. Japan's attack on Pearl Harbor in 1941 brought the United States directly into the conflict.

"Franklin Delano Roosevelt was a deeply religious man with a respect for all religions,"[1] writes his secretary who was familiar with almost every aspect of the president's life. This was the verdict also of all who knew him intimately. He was brought up in the Episcopal tradition and became an active vestryman and a senior warden of St. James's Church at Hyde Park. Because of physical disabilities during the entire period of his presidency he attended church only on special occasions at Hyde Park or in Washington, but his prayer book was never far from him and his Bible was often read.

One of the powerful influences on Roosevelt's life was the remarkable personality and Christian character of Dr. Endicott Peabody, rector and headmaster at Groton School. He laid great stress on manliness and personal integrity. At Roosevelt's urgent request he officiated at his wedding. Dr. Peabody also participated in the worship service at St. John's Episcopal Church, Washington, which the Roosevelt family attended prior to the inauguration. Roosevelt's first inaugural address ended with the fervent prayer: "We humbly ask the blessing of God. May he protect every one of us and guide me in the days to come."

Another factor in Roosevelt's religious life was his crippling illness. Eleanor Roosevelt writes: "Franklin's

[1] Grace Tully, *F.D.R., My Boss,* p. 296.

illness was another turning point and proved a blessing in disguise: for it gave him strength and courage he had not had before."[2]

After the President's death, Mrs. Roosevelt wrote: "I am quite sure that Franklin accepted the thought of death as he accepted life. He had a strong religious feeling and his religion was a very personal one. I think he actually felt he could ask God for guidance and receive it. That is why he loved the Twenty-third Psalm, the Beatitudes and the Thirteenth Chapter of First Corinthians. He never talked about his religion or his beliefs and never seemed to have any intellectual difficulties about what he believed."[3]

Eleanor Roosevelt's final comment on the subject sums it all up: "He still held to the fundamental feeling that religion was an anchor and a source of strength and guidance, so I am sure that he died looking into the future as calmly as he had looked at all the events of his life."[4]

So he passed from the American scene a highly controversial but powerful and wholly dedicated president.

[2] Eleanor Roosevelt, *This I Remember*, p. 25.

[3] *Ibid.*, p. 346.

[4] *Ibid.*, p. 347.

HARRY S. TRUMAN

HARRY S. TRUMAN

[1884–   ]

TEN PRESIDENTS OF THE UNITED STATES LACKED A COLLEGE education, one of whom was Harry Truman. Lack of funds prevented him from going to college and near-sightedness closed the doors of a military or naval academy. Indeed, because of difficulty in getting proper glasses fitted he did not begin school until he was eight years of age. However, his mother taught him his letters and he had begun reading before the age of five. Once again his eyes proved a handicap so far as strenuous games of boyhood were concerned. Since his special glasses did not lend themselves to sports, the time that might have been spent on strenuous play was given to worthwhile reading. He was especially engrossed with the biographies of American presidents.

"By the time I was thirteen or fourteen," writes Truman, "I had read all the books in the Independence Public Library and our big old Bible I had read three times through." [1]

Truman was born on May 8, 1884, in Lamar, Mis-

---

[1] Harry S. Truman, *Memoirs,* Vol. II, p. 116.

souri, the son of a small-time farmer. When Harry was six years old the family moved to Independence, where his father, John A. Truman, had purchased a farm. In his memoirs Truman speaks of 440 acres in one area and less than a hundred in another, "To play around in." But it was not all play. From his early years Harry had his daily chores to perform. Despite his late start in school he was regarded as a bright student and was graduated from high school at the age of seventeen.

When the United States entered World War I, Harry Truman went to France commissioned as a first lieutenant of artillery. Far removed from the shy recruit who began training, he proved in action to be a cool and competent leader. His first concern was the welfare of his men who responded with affection and admiration. Later he was promoted to captain. Truman himself tells us that his wartime training and testing gave him fresh confidence in himself and in his ability to lead men.

One manifestation of this new assurance in himself was his early engagement and marriage to a boyhood sweetheart, Bess Wallace. With an Army comrade he opened a haberdashery in Kansas City, but the venture failed and Truman assumed the debt of $20,000, which he paid off in the course of ten years, refusing to take the route of bankruptcy proceedings.

When his fortunes were at their lowest he was introduced to Thomas J. Pendergast, boss of the Democratic machine in Kansas City. He helped Truman to secure the post of presiding judge in Jackson County. After this came Truman's first big opportunity: election to the United States Senate in 1934. He was reelected without

213

the help of the Pendergast machine, which had totally collapsed, most of its stalwarts having been sent to prison.

During his second term in the Senate, Truman became interested in the creation of a strong watchdog committee to curb collusion and graft between Army officials and corporation executives in the new rearmament program. He was made chairman of the committee which did such a masterful job that the country was saved hundreds of millions of dollars. This gave Truman a national reputation for efficiency and integrity and caused Roosevelt to select him as his running mate in 1944. When Roosevelt died on April 12, 1945, Harry S. Truman was sworn in as president. His first act was to visit Mrs. Roosevelt.

"Is there anything I can do for you?" asked Truman.

She replied: "Is there anything we can do for you? You are the one in trouble now."[2]

Nothing could have been closer to the truth. He was in real trouble.

Here are some of the momentous happenings of his seven years' Administration and also a reminder of some of the history-making decisions that fell to his lot: putting into effect the terms of the German surrender, dropping the first atom bomb on Japan, arranging a huge postwar loan to Britain, effecting a major change of policy toward Russia, sending a large expeditionary force to Korea on behalf of the United Nations, dismissing General Douglas MacArthur. He refused to run for reelection in 1952.

Having served his country, this "hired man of 150 million people" as he liked to call himself, surrendered

[2] *Ibid.*, Vol. I, p. 5.

his responsibilities and like Cincinnatus, a hero of the old Roman republic, he retired to the seclusion of his homestead.

Truman avowed that, in his most difficult tasks and perplexing decisions, it was the inspiration and strength of his religious faith that carried him through.

While living in Independence, the Truman family, which had followed the Baptist tradition, attended a Presbyterian Church because it was close to their home. In Washington they affiliated with a Baptist Church, attending with unfailing regularity.[3] After he had been sworn in as president, after the death of Franklin Roosevelt, he was congratulated by a group of reporters. To them he said in deadly earnest that if they believed in prayer, to pray for him, for he needed it badly. He told them he felt as though the whole universe had fallen on him, the sun, the moon, and all the stars.[4]

President Truman's task was made far more difficult because people persisted in comparing him with his extraordinary predecessor from all points of view: education, social background, personal appearance, experience, and speaking ability. Yet even his most grudging critics are compelled to admit that he acquitted himself well and that for the most part his decisions were in the best interest of the American people.

In his first address as president to a joint session of Congress, Truman's demeanor was that of a modest but courageous man. He concluded with these words: "I ask only to be a good and faithful servant of my Lord and my people."

---

[3] *Ibid.*, p. 116.
[4] *Ibid.*, p. 19.

DWIGHT D. EISENHOWER

DWIGHT D. EISENHOWER

[1890–1969]

IT WAS A LONG WAY FROM THE HOME OF A GENERAL mechanic in the little town of Abilene, Kansas, where life was an unceasing struggle against poverty, to the post of general of the United States Army, commander in chief of the European Theater of Operations. and later president of the United States. Yet that was the road taken by Dwight David Eisenhower, one of six sons of David and Ida Eisenhower. Dwight, or "Ike," as he was nicknamed early in his life, was born in Denison, Texas, but when he was a few months old the family moved back to Kansas and settled in Abilene, where the Eisenhowers had formerly lived. Religion, hard work, and a meager income were for quite some years characteristic of their family life. The father was a mechanic in a creamery and the six boys raised vegetables, cut wood, and did any job that was available, turning over to their mother the cash they had earned.

The Eisenhowers belonged to a religious sect known as the River Brethren because they had settled by the Susquehanna River in Pennsylvania. The adherents of this religious fellowship were loosely associated with the larger grouping called Mennonites who were followers of Menno Simons, of Holland. At one time Mennonites were numerous and influential in the Netherlands. The River Brethren were inclined to fundamentalist theology, a very simple church organization, marked reverence for the Bible, passivism, and refusal to take an oath.

In Dwight Eisenhower's boyhood home the Bible was daily read at family devotions, each member of the family in turn reading the passage for the day. This practice had an educational as well as a religious value since any mistakes in reading were sharply corrected. To the very close of his life Dwight Eisenhower carried in his mind and heart the indelible imprint of his parents' religion. It was a severe blow to both the mother and father that he should choose for additional education the United States Military Academy at West Point, New York. They both recognized, however, that this move did not entail a breach, on the part of Dwight, with the centralities of his faith. After learning of his intention his mother said simply, "It's your decision." His brother Milton later told Ike that following this conversation he had heard his mother crying. It is possible, however, that her tears had as much or more to do with his leaving home as it had with the Academy.

Dwight Eisenhower's high school record was well above average despite many hours devoted to labor and school sports. During the year before West Point he worked in the Belle Springs Creamery, where his father labored as a mechanic.

At the military academy his record was in no way spectacular, but he evidenced a marked willingness to learn. His graduation standing was sixty-one in a class of well over double that number. He was popular with both instructors and comrades. After graduation, on July 1, 1916, he married Mamie Geneva Doud at her home in Denver, Colorado. During the period between the two world wars Ike served as commander in several important military posts and received the rating "S," for "superior."

After the outbreak of World War II, General George C. Marshall, chief of staff, called in Eisenhower for a talk and then appointed him assistant chief of the War Plans Division. Ike's grasp of global strategy impressed Marshall, who promoted him to major general (temporary). Eisenhower was now working on cross-channel invasion plans. He drew up a directive for the unnamed commander of the European theater. On what is one of the most memorable dates in Eisenhower's life, June 15, 1942, he laid the complete directive on General Marshall's desk. The general looked over the papers and then said to Ike, "Are you satisfied with them?" Eisenhower replied that he was. Marshall said that this was fine "because these are the orders you are to operate under; you're in command of the European Theatre of Operations." Ten days later Eisenhower had established his headquarters in London.[1]

At the victorious close of World War II, Eisenhower was one of the most popular leaders in the whole Western world. He was given tumultuous welcomes in Britain and in several strategic cities in the United States. Very shortly his name was heard in political circles, but his acceptance of the post of successor to Nicholas Murray Butler as president of Columbia University de-

[1] *Encyclopædia Britannica,* Vol. VIII, p. 114.

layed any action. In 1952, however, he ran as Republican candidate against the Democrat Adlai E. Stevenson. Ike won, carrying 39 states with a total of 442 electoral votes.

Early in the morning of January 20, 1953, Dwight D. Eisenhower, his wife, and family, joined by his Cabinet and the members of their families, made their way quietly to the National Presbyterian Church. That day Eisenhower was to be inaugurated as the nation's thirty-fourth president. Never before had the Cabinet members met with the president-elect in this type of service. The service opened with the historic and well-loved hymn "Our God, Our Help in Ages Past," and deeply moving prayers were said by the pastor Rev. Dr. Edward L. R. Elson. Eisenhower, quieted and inspired by the service, went back to his suite in the Statler Hotel to write the words of a prayer that he would read during the inaugural ceremonies. It was worded in part as follows: "Almighty God, give us, we pray thee, power to discern right from wrong, and allow our words and actions to be governed thereby and by the laws of this land. Especially we pray that our concern shall be for all the people, regardless of station, race, or calling, so that all may work for the good of our beloved country and thy glory. Amen."

Twelve days after the inauguration President Eisenhower was baptized and received into full membership in the National Presbyterian Church in Washington. Mrs. Eisenhower had been a lifelong Presbyterian and she joined the local church with the president.

A few mornings later the first of what has become known as the Presidential Prayer Breakfasts was held.

This series has been continued once a year without a break through the administrations of Presidents Kennedy, Johnson, and Nixon. The initial meeting was attended by Cabinet officers, members of Congress, the judiciary, businessmen, and religious leaders.

President Eisenhower witnessed to the power of prayer in his life. He testified that prayer put him in touch with the Infinite and, by opening his mind and heart to God, he found divine energies flowing through him, with which he could undertake his duties and solve his problems. He commented on several instances in his own life which confirmed his abiding faith in prayer and commended to others the way of prayer.[2]

Another distinct innovation was the practice of opening each Cabinet meeting with silent prayer. This move was strongly backed by Ezra T. Benson, secretary of agriculture, who was a Mormon.

Despite two severe illnesses, a thrombosis and ileitis, Eisenhower ran for a second term of office. He received in 1956 a considerable increase in both the popular and the electoral vote over that registered in 1952. His personal popularity remained undiminished.

Several presidents who had preceded Eisenhower, contemplated uniting with the church of their choice but deferred the move while serving as president in case the charge of "hypocrisy" would be flung at them. Among these were Andrew Jackson, James K. Polk, and James Buchanan. Eisenhower decided to ignore this risk, which in his case was not great for two reasons: first, his tremendous hold on the American people, and second, the people's belief in the genuineness of his professed faith.

[2] Frances Brentano (ed.), *Nation Under God.*

President Eisenhower by the goodwill which he engendered united the American people and by his freely acknowledged faith in God warmed their hearts, leaving us with the memory of a great and good man. He died March 28, 1969.

JOHN F. KENNEDY

JOHN F. KENNEDY

[1917–1963]

FEW INDEED AMONG THE CANDIDATES FOR THE PRESIDENCY
of the United States have been faced with such formidable obstacles to his success as John Fitzgerald Kennedy.
The greatest barrier of all, and by many people thought
to be insuperable, was the fact of his Roman Catholicism. Only one Catholic politician before him sought
this office, Alfred E. Smith, and he went down to overwhelming defeat. (Of course he might have been defeated even if he had not been a Roman Catholic.) A
second obstacle was Kennedy's youth. But, he had already demonstrated his vote-getting powers on two occasions. In 1947 he was elected a United States congressman and five years later he ran successfully for the
Senate against so stalwart an opponent as Henry Cabot
Lodge, Jr., who had been Eisenhower's campaign manager. Despite these notable victories people still commented on his youthful appearance on television and
questioned "sending a boy on a man's journey."

On the other hand, John Kennedy had undeniable assets. He was superbly educated in Choate Preparatory

School and Harvard University, from which he was graduated *cum laude*. He had also taken postgraduate work at the London School of Economics and Stanford University, California. His major interest had always been political science. After the death of his brother Joseph, who had political life in view but was killed in action in World War II, John stepped forward to take his place.

During the period when his father, Joseph P. Kennedy, was ambassador to the Court of St. James (1937–1940) his family, including John, lived in the American Embassy, London. The elder Kennedy wrote pessimistic letters to Roosevelt, painting a gloomy picture of England's future, and declared in one of them that in the face of Adolf Hitler's onslaught "England didn't have a Chinaman's chance."

Roosevelt did not agree with his ambassador's gloomy predictions and wrote: "While the World War did not bring forth strong leadership in Great Britain this war may do so [He was probably thinking of Churchill], because I am inclined to think that the British public has more humility than before and is slowly but surely getting rid of the 'muddle through' attitude of the past." [1] One hopes that Joseph Kennedy was a better ambassador than he was a prophet! Robert Burns wrote:

> "A chiel's amang you takin' notes,
> And faith he'll prent it." [2]

---

[1] Elliott Roosevelt and others (eds.), *F. D. R.: His Personal Letter, 1928–1945*, pp. 449–450.
[2] Robert Burns, "On the Late Captain Grose's Peregrinations thro' Scotland."

The "chiel" in this case was young John Kennedy, twenty-three years old. He took ample notes and print them he did! The book was titled *Why England Slept*. It was a far more perceptive appraisal of the international situation and England's plight in particular than his father's. He was careful, however, not to embarrass his father in what he had written. This book actually was his Harvard thesis which won him *cum laude*. Written in a more popular form, it sold well in Britain and in the United States.

When John Kennedy got the presidency clearly in his "sights" he started to solicit votes actively and earnestly. The religious issue he faced head on and with disarming candor.

Probably the most crucial encounter with the electorate on this theme took place in Houston, Texas, where he accepted an invitation to address a large group of Protestant ministers. There was genuine fear among these ministers that with the advent of a Roman Catholic president there would soon be direct interference of the Roman hierarchy in American political affairs. This nettle Kennedy firmly grasped. He said, in part:

"I believe in an America where the separation of Church and State is absolute, where no Catholic prelate would tell the President (should he be a Catholic) how to act and no Protestant minister would tell his parishioners for whom to vote. . . .

"I believe in an America where no religious body seeks to impose its will directly or indirectly upon the general populace or the public acts of its officials. . . .

"But if this election is decided on the basis that 40,000,000 Americans lost their chance of being president on the day they were baptized, then it is the whole nation that will be the loser in the eyes of Catholics and non-Catholics around the world, in the eyes of history, and in the eyes of our own people." [3]

This address and the answers to questions asked later in this meeting drew forth sympathetic applause. Kennedy was elected by the smallest plurality given a victor in any presidential election, certainly in this century.

Theodore G. Sorensen, dealing with Kennedy's promises to his constituents, writes: "True to his word he showed no religious favoritism in the selection of his appointees, no fear of ecclesiastical pressures and no divided loyalty of any kind. No ambassador was sent to the Vatican. With his support the federal government quietly but extensively increased its activities in the area of birth control and population control. Having told the Texas preachers that he would have no hesitancy in attending a Protestant service in his capacity as President, he flew in his first year to Texas for the funeral of Sam Rayburn. He attended Prayer Breakfasts with Billy Graham." [4]

Looking back over the life of John Kennedy and especially his all too brief tenure of the presidency, we see a man whose moral and spiritual stature ranks him among the greatest of our presidents even though his powers had not yet been fully matured. He made mistakes as all presidents have done. One of the worst was the Bay of Pigs fiasco. But one achievement towers above any others during the whole of his Administration—the Cuban missile crisis. Even now, years later,

[3] Press report, *The New York Times.*
[4] Theodore C. Sorensen, *Kennedy,* p. 364.

one cannot read the biographer's account of Kennedy's behavior in those thirteen suspenseful days when the nations of the world "peered over the rim of hell" without unbounded admiration for Kennedy's wisdom, his restraint and self-control, his firmness and courage, which stayed the hand of Nikita Khrushchev and put fear into the heart of a ruthless aggressor. We can pay no finer tribute to John Fitzgerald Kennedy than the words of eulogy spoken by Edmund Burke of Charles James Fox (who became an English member of Parliament at the age of nineteen): "He may live long, he may do much. But here is the summit. He never can exceed what he does this day." [5]

John Kennedy did not live long, but he lived long enough to make an enduring place for himself in the hearts of his fellow countrymen.

----

[5] Quoted by Sorensen in *Kennedy*, p. 718.

LYNDON B. JOHNSON

LYNDON B. JOHNSON

[1908–   ]

SINCE THE COMMENCEMENT OF THE TWENTIETH CENTURY four vice-presidents of the United States, most of them with little or no warning, have been suddenly thrust into the presidency. These were Theodore Roosevelt, Calvin Coolidge, Harry Truman, and Lyndon Johnson. A question of vital concern for each of these vice-presidents was, "How much time have I left to develop a program and 'prove' myself before I must go to the electorate for a mandate to be president in my own right?" Lyndon Johnson faced a more difficult task than any of the other three, for an interval of only eleven or twelve months remained before the next election. In addition, the circumstances of President Kennedy's death were so shocking and brutal and the recollections of his youthfulness, vigor, and forthgoing friendliness were still so clear and strong that any successor, no matter how capable, must, for a time at least, suffer by comparison and also from a measure of unreasoning resentment.

For some months after assuming the presidency Lyndon Johnson retained much of the staff assembled by John Kennedy. Some of these mistakenly thought that out of loyalty to their former chief they should be reluctant to serve his successor. On the evening of his return from Dallas, Johnson asked for two sheets of presidential stationery. When the request was made to a Kennedy aide the notepaper was handed over sullenly with the remark: "The body not cold yet—and he's grabbing for the President's stationery." What the Kennedy aide did not know was that Lyndon Johnson wanted the stationery so that his first letters as president of the United States would be handwritten notes to Caroline and John John Kennedy.[1]

Lyndon Baines Johnson was born August 27, 1908, near Stonewall, Texas. His higher education was acquired at Southwest Texas State Teachers College at San Marcos, where he received his B.S. degree in 1930. For two years thereafter he taught school in Houston. In late 1932, Johnson journeyed to Washington to serve as secretary to a Texas Congressman. On moving to Washington, he used every spare moment in studying law at Georgetown University.

On November 17, 1934, after a whirlwind courtship he married Claudia Alta Taylor, known to everyone as "Lady Bird." They had two daughters, Lynda Bird and Luci Baines.

Learning that a congressional seat in Texas had become vacant through the death of its occupant in 1936, Lyndon Johnson determined to enter the political race against nine aspirants, some of whom were experienced candidates. The sum of $10,000 was required. This money was immediately provided by Mrs. Johnson's father T. J. Taylor, who was a man of considerable

[1] Eric F. Goldman, *The Tragedy of Lyndon Baines Johnson,* p. 19.

means. By dint of stupendous and well-organized canvassing Lyndon Johnson won the seat. From that moment onward he never turned his eyes away from a shining goal that loomed before him—the presidency. On the way, he spent twelve years in the House of Representatives. In 1948 he was elected to the United States Senate, very shortly making his presence felt in that body. Elected leader by his Democratic colleagues in 1953, he was recognized on all sides as a master of persuasion and compromise.

The foundation of Lyndon Johnson's wealth was laid in 1942 when radio station KTBC went up for sale. Because it was in poor repair and badly managed it could be bought for $30,000. Once again "Dad" Taylor lent a helping hand. The Johnsons got a rare bargain which paid off handsomely just as the television era was opening.

The Johnsons are a sincerely religious family. Lady Bird has a strong Episcopal background, and although she attended churches of other denominations with the president, she steadfastly retained her Episcopal affiliation. Lyndon Johnson's mother was a Baptist, but the president from early years belonged to the Disciples of Christ, or Christian Church. Lyndon Johnson has attended churches of many denominations in Washington, but his home church is a small Disciples chapel in Johnson City, Texas. Their daughters followed the family pattern until Luci, the younger, shortly before her marriage to Patrick J. Nugent converted to Roman Catholicism.

On Saturday, May 13, 1967, a story appeared in *The New York Times,* page 1, under the byline of Max Frankel. It had been run in two Washington papers the previous day. It appears that President Johnson had previously told it in intimate circles many times. Now it had hit the press. It is worth recording for the light it sheds on the president's personality. As Johnson tells it, Luci came in late on the evening of June 29, 1966, and found her father tired and worried. She asked the reason why. Her father replied that he had authorized a bombing raid near the center of Hanoi and Haiphong. It was estimated that some ten planes would be lost and he feared lest a Russian ship might be hit or other grave incident occur. He quoted himself as saying: "Your daddy may go down in history as having started World War III." Luci thereupon suggested that she and the president should visit her "little monks" at St. Dominic's Chapel a mile and a half from the White House. Even though it was midnight, the president ordered a secret service limousine and made the journey. On their return the president had a short nap but couldn't sleep long because reports of the raid were coming in all night. All planes were on target. No serious complications ensued. Only one plane was down and the pilot was saved. When the final reports were in, the president, reassured, went to bed and slept late the next morning. Luci was jubilant. "My little monks usually come through," she said. In telling the story, the president stressed not so much his midnight visit to the chapel as the comfort of having an affectionate daughter who shared his burden.

President Johnson, when assured that ministers of his own denomination, in convention assembled, and other Christian friends were praying for him, remarked: "No man could live in the house where I live and work at the desk where I work without needing and seeking the support of earnest and frequent prayer. Prayer has helped me to bear the burdens of the first office, which are too great to be borne by anyone alone."

President Johnson's goal of the "Great Society" and the achievements of his Administration in social advance and civil rights became increasingly obscured by the escalation of the Vietnam war. Vast sums of money diverted from urgent domestic problems; young Americans in steadily mounting numbers dying amid the jungles and rice paddies of Southeast Asia; helpless civilian men, women, and children suffering untold miseries; these frustrating and brutal happenings had their beginning in the regimes of three earlier presidents and were inherited by Lyndon Johnson. They reached a crescendo, however, during his Administration, bringing down upon his head vilification and a storm of hate such as few presidents of this nation have had to endure.

In a dramatic television announcement, March 31, 1968, President Johnson surprised the nation by stating that in the hope of opening a doorway to fresh negotiations that could bring peace in Southeast Asia, he would eliminate himself by neither seeking nor accepting renomination for the presidency. This totally unexpected move on the part of the president produced a wave of sympathetic understanding of the tremendously difficult role he had filled for some five or six years.

We are too close to the Administration of Lyndon Johnson to reach a clear and just estimate of its success or failure. For this we must await the verdict of history.

RICHARD M. NIXON

RICHARD M. NIXON
[1913–   ]

PRESIDENT NIXON, LIKE HIS PREDECESSOR HERBERT HOOVER, has a religious background in the Society of Friends. Although he is a birthright Quaker who still maintains his membership in the Friends' Meeting, East Whittier, California, Nixon finds it easy to worship in churches of any Christian denomination. Indeed, he appears to prefer a Protestant style of worship conducted by a minister to the unprogrammed worship of the Quaker tradition. Nixon inherited his Quaker faith from his mother. She was a strong pacifist and an equally determined believer in civil liberty. There were five sons in the family, two of whom died in early life. When one of the boys contracted tuberculosis his mother took him to Arizona in the hope of a better climate for healing. She paid their board by washing, scrubbing, and cooking. Nixon's father's income from his small general store did not suffice to maintain the family without the help of the boys. Richard's jobs included janitor of a swimming pool, barker at a rodeo, and helper in a packinghouse. These odd jobs were not allowed to interfere with his schoolwork in which he ranked high. His special interest was debating and oratory contests. The politician was already beginning to emerge.

A number of our presidents were born in homes where life was a long struggle with want. In this battle for a livelihood they built resolute character that stood them in good stead in later years. Among such presidents were Jackson, Van Buren, Fillmore, Lincoln, Andrew Johnson, Garfield, Cleveland, Truman, Eisenhower, Lyndon Johnson, and Nixon.

Richard Milhous Nixon was born in the farming community of Yorba Linda some thirty miles from Los Angeles on January 9, 1913. He was graduated in 1934 from Whittier College, where he majored in constitutional history, and from Duke University Law School in 1937. During World War II he served four years in the Navy, leaving it with the rank of lieutenant commander.

Winning the Twelfth Congressional District of California in 1946, Nixon returned to the United States Congress without opposition in 1948. While there he helped to draft and enact the Taft-Hartley Labor Relations Act. Richard Nixon's name came to the attention of the nation because of the active role he played in exposing the Communist affiliation of Alger Hiss, later convicted of perjury. In 1950 after a bitter contest he was elected junior senator from California.

The first long stride toward the presidency took place in 1952 when he was nominated as running mate of Dwight D. Eisenhower and elected by a large majority. During the campaign his opponents charged that he had illegally used a fund raised by his supporters. So vigorously were the charges pressed that even some of the top leadership of the Republican Party began to discuss his withdrawal from the campaign. Nixon decided to answer the charges in a television broadcast heard by millions of Americans. He frankly revealed his financial situation, withholding nothing, and appealed for his listeners' verdict. So overwhelmingly favorable was the response that within twenty-four hours Nixon had become one of the most favored candidates. He later confessed that he had been immeasurably strengthened by a telegram from his Quaker mother. It simply said: "Keep the faith."

Having won the election, President Eisenhower urged his vice-president to reinvigorate this neglected office, which he proceeded to do. He was frequently an articulate spokesman for the Administration. He presided at meetings of the Cabinet and the National Security Council in the absence of the president. He mediated labor-management disputes.

Now a new and most important assignment fell to his lot. He was requested by the president to travel throughout the world as an ambassador of American goodwill. His wife, Patricia, accompanied him. For the most part his reception in various countries was cordial. In Caracas, Venezuela, however, a very dangerous situation developed. The Communists in Caracas were well acquainted with Richard Nixon's reputation as a foe of Marxism, and a plot was actually hatched for his assassination. On the day he was scheduled to lay a wreath at the tomb of Bolivar, the Nixon procession was halted and blocked by trucks and buses and a concerted attack was made on the vice-president's car. Instantly it became a target for rocks, bottles, iron pipes, and some explosives. The United States flags were torn from all cars and trampled in the streets. So great was the rain of spittle on the Nixon car that the driver had to use his windshield wiper. At one stage the vice-president stepped from the car and moved into the mob. This action on his part so startled the aggressors that they moved backward. When Nixon returned to the car the mob began to rock it violently with the purpose of overturning it and setting it on fire. With great calmness and courage the president ordered the driver to start the engine and drive down a side street to the American Embassy. The alert secret service forced a way for the autos and they drove swiftly to shelter and safety where armed Marines were on guard.

Later it was learned that the American wreath sent to the Bolivar monument was torn into shreds and that a car loaded with homemade bombs was awaiting the vice-president's arrival.

The following day the American Embassy was deluged with flowers and apologies from the provisional president of Venezuela and his Cabinet. Law-abiding citizens deeply regretted the rioting. It was said by American reporters that no man could have shown greater courage than did Pat Nixon during those perilous hours on the streets of Caracas. When a few days later the vice-president's plane landed at the National Airport, Washington, a crowd of fifteen thousand persons were there to honor the heroic travelers and, laying protocol aside, President Eisenhower was one of the first to greet Vice-President Nixon and Mrs. Nixon, followed by his entire Cabinet.

In July, 1959, the vice-president flew to Moscow to open the first American Exposition ever held there. The Soviet Premier, Nikita Khrushchev, decided to test the mettle of the vice-president in what has become known as the "Kitchen Debate." Fortunately Nixon came to Moscow thoroughly prepared for just such an encounter and acquitted himself well and put the case for American democracy in an appealing light to the Russian people. Later American Ambassador Thompson said to Nixon, "Five years ago it would have been absolutely unthinkable for anyone to say the things you did to the Russian people."[1]

Nominated for the presidency in 1960 by the Republican Convention, Nixon was defeated in the election by a very small majority by Senator John Fitzgerald Kennedy. Later he lost out in the election for governor of California.

After Nixon had suffered the dual defeats and especially following his blistering attack upon the press of the nation, the news media were ready to write him off as a political liability. But these persons seriously underrated the inner resources of Richard Nixon and his stubborn determination to press toward the presidential goal. For several years he was seldom visible in political circles, seeming to confirm the gloomy predictions with respect to his future. But during all these months he was quietly at work preparing himself for a renewed drive toward his lifetime objective. Meticulous preparation had always been his method, and never was this more true than in the '60s prior to the Republican Convention of 1968. He was exemplifying Ovid's dictum in *Metamorphosis*: "And though he greatly failed, more greatly dared."

In 1968, Nixon won the nomination of the Republican Convention and went on to win the presidency. The

[1] Richard M. Nixon, *Six Crises*, chapter on Khrushchev.

following January he found himself leading a nation that was rent asunder by sharp differences of opinion on the Vietnam war, agitated by legitimate protest which was constantly provoked into mob violence by well-trained groups of anarchists and revolutionists. It was a crisis situation. Earl Mazo, Richard Nixon's biographer, has written significantly: "Nixon is at his best in a crisis." [2]

At this juncture the American public might well have remembered the tribute paid to Nixon by President Eisenhower when Ike was struck down by a heart attack and it looked as if the vice-president at any moment might be called upon to succeed him: "There is no man in the history of America who has had such careful preparation for carrying out the duties of the Presidency." [3]

President Nixon has put more emphasis on the occasional religious service in the White House than any other chief executive since the practice was begun by President Rutherford Hayes. It is now a truly ecumenical meeting with a more formal structure than heretofore.

The president also attended and addressed the Presidential Prayer Breakfast, which had its commencement during the Eisenhower Administration. H. H. Haldeman, presidential assistant who sees Nixon on an hour-to-hour basis, has said, "The President is a very deeply religious man." [4]

Billy Graham, a friend of the Nixons for two decades, has also testified to the strength of the president's faith

[2] Earl Mazo, *Richard Nixon: A Political and Personal Portrait,* p. 4.
[3] *Ibid.,* p. 188.
[4] *The Christian Science Monitor,* Dec. 20, 1969.

and added, "But he doesn't wear his religion on his sleeve." [5]

President Nixon in a brief, impromptu talk at the Prayer Breakfast referred to earlier, confessed that he, like many a president before him, had been fortified and sustained in his heavy responsibilities by his Christian faith. He concluded with words reminiscent of Abraham Lincoln: "There has to be something more than honesty and wisdom in the leadership of this country. There are times when we need help beyond ourselves, beyond what any man can give us, in order to make the right decision for this nation." [6]

---

[5] *Ibid.*
[6] *The Christian Science Monitor Herald,* Feb., 1970.

PRESIDENTIAL PROFILES

	President	Chronology	Religion	Education	In Office
1.	GEORGE WASHINGTON	1732–1799	Episcopal	No college	1789–1797
2.	JOHN ADAMS	1735–1826	Attended Episcopal	Harvard	1797–1801
3.	THOMAS JEFFERSON	1743–1826	Attended Episcopal	William and Mary	1801–1809
4.	JAMES MADISON	1751–1836	Attended Episcopal	Princeton	1809–1817
5.	JAMES MONROE	1758–1831	Episcopal	William and Mary	1817–1825
6.	JOHN QUINCY ADAMS	1767–1848	Independent Congregational	Harvard	1825–1829
7.	ANDREW JACKSON	1767–1845	Presbyterian	No college	1829–1837
8.	MARTIN VAN BUREN	1782–1862	Dutch Reformed	No college	1837–1841
9.	WILLIAM HENRY HARRISON	1773–1841	Attended Episcopal	Hampden-Sydney	1841–1841
10.	JOHN TYLER	1790–1862	Episcopal	William and Mary	1841–1845
11.	JAMES K. POLK	1795–1849	Presbyterian and Methodist	University of North Carolina	1845–1849
12.	ZACHARY TAYLOR	1784–1850	Attended Episcopal	No college	1849–1850
13.	MILLARD FILLMORE	1800–1874	Unitarian	No college	1850–1853

Continued on page 246

14.	Franklin Pierce	1804–1869	Episcopal	Bowdoin	1853–1857
15.	James Buchanan	1791–1868	Presbyterian	Dickinson	1857–1861
16.	Abraham Lincoln	1809–1865	Attended Presbyterian and other churches	No college	1861–1865
17.	Andrew Johnson	1808–1875	Attended many churches	No college	1865–1869
18.	Ulysses S. Grant	1822–1885	Attended Methodist	West Point	1869–1877
19.	Rutherford B. Hayes	1822–1893	Attended Methodist	Kenyon and Harvard	1877–1881
20.	James A. Garfield	1831–1881	Disciples of Christ	Williams	1881–1881
21.	Chester A. Arthur	1830–1886	Attended Baptist and Episcopal	Union College, Schenectady	1881–1885
22.	Grover Cleveland	1837–1908	Presbyterian	No college	1885–1889
23.	Benjamin Harrison	1833–1901	Presbyterian	Miami of Ohio	1889–1893
24.	Grover Cleveland	1837–1908	Presbyterian	No college	1893–1897
25.	William McKinley	1843–1901	Methodist Episcopal	Allegheny	1897–1901
26.	Theodore Roosevelt	1858–1919	Dutch Reformed	Harvard	1901–1909
27.	William Howard Taft	1857–1930	Unitarian	Yale	1909–1913
28.	Woodrow Wilson	1856–1924	Presbyterian	Princeton	1913–1921
29.	Warren G. Harding	1865–1923	Baptist	Ohio Central	1921–1923

30.	CALVIN COOLIDGE	1872–1933	Congregational	Amherst	1923–1929
31.	HERBERT C. HOOVER	1874–1964	Society of Friends	Stanford	1929–1933
32.	FRANKLIN D. ROOSEVELT	1882–1945	Episcopal	Harvard	1933–1945
33.	HARRY S. TRUMAN	1884–	Baptist	No college	1945–1953
34.	DWIGHT D. EISENHOWER	1890–1969	Presbyterian	West Point	1953–1961
35.	JOHN F. KENNEDY	1917–1963	Roman Catholic	Harvard	1961–1963
36.	LYNDON B. JOHNSON	1908–	Christian (Disciples of Christ)	Southwest Texas State Teachers	1963–1969
37.	RICHARD M. NIXON	1913–	Society of Friends	Whittier	1969–

BIBLIOGRAPHY

Adams, Charles Francis (ed.), *The Memoirs of John Quincy Adams*. 12 vols. J. B. Lippincott Company, 1876–1877.

Adams, James Truslow, *The Adams Family*. Little, Brown and Company, 1930.

Adams, Samuel Hopkins, *The Incredible Era: The Life and Times of Warren Gamaliel Harding*. Houghton Mifflin Company, 1939.

Baker, Ray Stannard, and Dodd, William E. (eds.), *The Public Papers*. (Woodrow Wilson) 1925.

Barnard, Harry, *Rutherford Hayes and His America*. The Bobbs-Merrill Company, Inc.

Bassett, John Spencer, *The Life of Andrew Jackson*. The Macmillan Company, 1916.

Black, Harold Garnet, *The True Woodrow Wilson, Crusader for Democracy*. Fleming H. Revell Company, 1946.

Brentano, Frances (ed.), *Nation Under God*. Channel Press, 1957.

Bunyan, John, *The Pilgrim's Progress*.

Burns, Robert, "On the Late Captain Grose's Peregrinations thro' Scotland."

Cleaves, Freeman, *Old Tippecanoe, William Henry Harrison and His Times*. Charles Scribner's Sons, 1939.

Coolidge, Calvin, *The Autobiography of.* Cosmopolitan Book Corporation, 1929.

Coolridge, Louis A., *Ulysses S. Grant.* Houghton Mifflin Company, 1917.

Cousins, Norman, *In God We Trust.* Harper & Brothers, 1958.

Cranston, Ruth, *Woodrow Wilson.* Simon and Schuster, Inc., 1945.

Curtis, George Ticknor, *The Life of James Buchanan.* 2 vols. Harper & Brothers, 1883.

Dictionary of American Biography. Charles Scribner's Sons, 1928.

Dulce, Berton, and Richter, Edward J., *Religion and the Presidency.* The Macmillan Company, 1962.

Eckenrode, H. J., *Rutherford Hayes, Statesman of Reunion.* Dodd, Mead & Company, Inc., 1930.

Encyclopædia Britannica. 14th edition, 1962.

Freud, Sigmund, and Bullitt, William C., *Thomas Woodrow Wilson: A Psychological Study.* Houghton Mifflin Company, 1967.

Fuller, Edmund, and Green, David, *God in the White House.* Crown Publishers, Inc., 1968.

Goldman, Eric F., *The Tragedy of Lyndon Baines Johnson.* Alfred A. Knopf, Inc., 1969.

Grant, Ulysses S., *Personal Memoirs.* 2 vols. Charles L. Webster, New York, 1885.

Hamilton, Holman, *Zachary Taylor.* 2 vols. The Bobbs-Merrill Company, Inc., 1951.

Hampton, Vernon, *The Religious Background of the White House.* Christopher Publishing House, 1932.

Hayes, Rutherford, *Life* (Diary and Letters). 2 vols. Houghton Mifflin Company, 1914.

Hesseltine, William B., *Ulysses S. Grant.* Dodd, Mead & Company, Inc., 1935.

Hinshaw, David, *Herbert Hoover: American Guide.*

———— *Herbert Hoover: American Quaker.* Farrar, Straus and Co., 1950.

Hoover, Herbert, *Memoirs, 1929–1941.* 3 vols. The Macmillan Company, 1952.

Isely, Bliss, *Presidents: Men of Faith.* W. A. Wilde Company, 1953.

Kellogg, Vernon, *Herbert Hoover, The Man and His Work.* D. Appleton & Company, 1920.

Leech, Margaret, *In the Days of McKinley.* Harper & Brothers, 1959.

Lynch, Denis Tilden, *A Man Four-Square.* Horace Liveright, Inc.

McElroy, Robert, *Grover Cleveland, The Man and the Statesman.* Harper & Brothers, 1923.

Mazo, Earl, *Richard Nixon: A Political and Personal Portrait.* Harper & Brothers, 1959.

National Intelligencer. Article on William Henry Harrison, April 13, 1841.

Nevins, Allan, *Grover Cleveland, A Story of Courage.* Dodd, Mead & Company, Inc., 1932.

Nichols, Roy Franklin, *Franklin Pierce: Young Hickory of the Granite Hills.* University of Pennsylvania Press, 1931.

Nixon, Richard M., *Six Crises.* Doubleday & Company, Inc., 1962.

Olcott, Charles S., *The Life of William McKinley.* 2 vols. Houghton Mifflin Company, 1916.

Oxford Dictionary of the Christian Church, The. London: Oxford University Press, 1958.

Padover, Saul (ed.), *A Jefferson Profile.* The John Day Company, 1956.

Parton, James, *Life of Andrew Jackson.* 3 vols. Ticknor and Fields, 1866.

Quaife, Milo Milton (ed.), *The Diary of James K. Polk.* 4 vols. A. C. McClurg & Company, Chicago, 1910.

Rives, William C., *Life and Times of James Madison.* 3 vols. Little, Brown and Company, 1859.

Roosevelt, Eleanor, *This I Remember*. Harper & Brothers, 1949.

Roosevelt, Elliott, and others (eds.), *F. D. R.: His Personal Letters*, 1928–1945. Duell, Sloan & Pearce, Inc., 1950.

Ross, Ishbel, *The General's Wife*. Dodd, Mead & Company, Inc., 1959.

Rosten, Leo (ed.), *The Religions of America*. London: William Heinemann, 1957.

Sandburg, Carl, *Abraham Lincoln: The War Years*. 4 vols. Harcourt, Brace & Company, Inc., 1939.

Sherwood, Robert E., *Roosevelt and Hopkins*. Harper & Brothers, 1948.

Sievers, Harry J., *Benjamin Harrison, Hoosier Warrior*. Henry Regnery Company, 1952.

Sinclair, Andrew, *The Available Man: The Life Behind the Masks of Warren Gamaliel Harding*. The Macmillan Company, 1965.

Smith, Margaret Bayard, *The First Forty Years of Washington Society*, ed. by Gaillard Hunt. Frederick Ungar Publishing Company, 1965.

Smith, Theodore Clarke, *The Life and Letters of James Abram Garfield*. 2 vols. Yale University Press, 1925.

Sorensen, Theodore C., *Kennedy*. Harper & Row, Publishers, Inc., 1965.

Todd, Helen, *A Man Named Grant*. Houghton Mifflin Company, 1940.

Truman, Harry S., *Memoirs*. 2 vols. Doubleday & Company, Inc., 1956.

Tully, Grace, *F. D. R., My Boss*. Charles Scribner's Sons, 1949.

Walworth, Arthur, *Woodrow Wilson* (Vol. I, American Prophet). Houghton Mifflin Company, 1958.

Weiss, Benjamin, *God in American History*. Zondervan Publishing House, 1966.

Williams, Charles R., *Letters and Diary of Rutherford Birchard Hayes*. 5 vols. Houghton Mifflin Company, 1914.

Williams, T. H. (ed.), *Hayes, The Diary of a President.* David McKay Company, Inc., 1964.

Wisconsin State Journal, July 10, 1884.

Wolf, William J., *The Religion of Abraham Lincoln.* The Seabury Press, Inc., 1963.

Wood, Frederick S., *Roosevelt as We Knew Him.* John C. Winston Company.